APPLYING THE STRATEGIC PERSPECTIVE

PROBLEMS AND MODELS

Fourth Edition

Leanne C. Powner
American University

CQ PRESS

A Division of SAGE
Washington, D.C.

CQ Press
2300 N Street, NW, Suite 800
Washington, DC 20037

Phone: 202-729-1900; toll-free, 1-866-427-7737 (1-866-4CQ-PRESS)

Web: www.cqpress.com

Cover design: Cynthia Richardson, RICHdesign Studio
Composition: C&M Digitals (P) Ltd.

♾ The paper used in this publication exceeds the requirements of the American National Standard for Information Sciences—Permanence of Paper for Printed Library Materials, ANSI Z39.48-1992.

Printed and bound in the United States of America

13   12   11   10   2   3   4   5

ISBN: 978-0-87289-611-6

Contents

TABLES AND FIGURES

Figures

NOTE TO STUDENTS

As you may have already discovered, the fourth edition of *Principles of International Politics* is a unique international relations textbook. Like other introductory texts, it attempts to give you a wide-ranging view of the field and its impressive body of scholarship. Yet, unlike most textbooks, *Principles* challenges you to analyze real political problems in a rigorous fashion using mathematical tools. Although the text will take you step by step through these analytic tools, applying them effectively requires practice. *Applying the Strategic Perspective* will help you do just that. It offers additional explanations, examples, and exercises to help you employ important theoretical concepts and technical skills. You will not find instruction for every subsection of every chapter of *Principles*. Instead, the workbook offers advice, information, and help on the text's most important technical methods, including:

- Additional "how to" explanations of technical material, such as how to solve a game by backwards induction;
- Additional examples that illustrate critical technical concepts;
- More information about the examples discussed in the text to provide further clarification of these materials;
- Problems and exercises to work through specific techniques, such as spatial modeling; and
- Opportunities to apply these techniques to real-world political problems.

HOW TO USE THIS BOOK

This is a book that is meant to be used—written in, scribbled on, and eventually torn up. As you work, you will find that you will need colored pens or pencils or highlighters and a simple calculator such as the ones on most cell phones or computers to solve some of the problems in this workbook. After you have worked through and solved exercises, your instructor may ask you to submit certain pages as homework. The workbook's pages are perforated to make this easy. We have endeavored to leave the space necessary for you to work right in the workbook, but in some cases, you may need more space to solve a problem than is provided. Should this occur, do your work on a separate sheet, write the answer in the workbook, and attach the sheet to the assignment. In other cases, you may simply want to follow along through the workbook as you read corresponding sections of the main text.

In general, when you see mathematical work in the text, you should consider working through the math alongside the text, and/or consulting this workbook for additional explanation. On the text's Web site, http://bdm .cqpress.com, you'll find a Math Appendix that reviews all the major concepts that you'll need as you read *Principles* and solve the workbook problems. Don't let the math worry you: *Principles* uses absolutely no math beyond what the SAT and ACT cover. Whereas most textbooks are designed to be read with a highlighter in hand, this one works best with a pencil and notebook paper for working through the examples on your own. It is important that you feel comfortable using the technical methods as they are introduced because you will be asked to apply them again in later sections of the book. The examples and exercises on these pages should help as you become familiar with the tools of *Principles* and allow you to gain a deeper understanding of the strategic perspective in international relations. Don't be shy, though. Be sure to ask your instructor to clarify any point you do not understand.

FOUNDATIONS OF INTERNATIONAL POLITICS

KEY CONCEPTS

Exercise I-1.   *Theories, Titles, and Assumptions*

The titles below are actual books and articles in international relations. Based on the title alone, indicate on the line whether you think the article or book has a Neorealist (NR), Liberal (L), or Constructivist (C) approach to international relations.

a)   "Cooperation under Anarchy" __*L*__

b)   "Normative Power Europe" __*C*__

c)   "The False Promise of International Institutions" _____

d)   "Anarchy Is What States Make of It" _____

e)   *Ruling the World: Power Politics and the Rise of Supranational Institutions* _____

f)   "Between Regimes and Realism—Transnational Agenda Setting: Soviet Compliance with CSCE Human Rights Norms" _____

g)   "State Power and International Trade" _____

h)   "Why Comply? Social Learning and European Identity Change" _____

Exercise I-2.   *Core Arguments*

This chapter makes three important arguments about international politics. For each argument, consider these corresponding questions.

Argument 1: Leaders take actions—both domestic and international—because they want to stay in power.

Give an example of a leader taking an international action that, in your view, contributed to his or her retaining power. Give an example of a leader taking an international (or domestic) action that contributed to his or her losing power. What else, besides retaining personal power, might motivate leaders to act in certain ways?

_____

_____

_____

_____

_____

Argument 2: International relations cannot be separated from domestic politics or from foreign policy.

What are some domestic political factors that might affect international political actions or choices? Give an example of one of these factors affecting the foreign policy of your country. What are some international political factors that might affect domestic political actions or choices? Again, give a brief example from your country.

_____

_____

_____

_____

_____

Argument 3: Relations between nations and between leaders are driven by reasoned decision making and strategic considerations.

Think about some actions your country's leader has recently taken in international politics.

a)   What are some alternative actions the leader could have taken in these situations, but did not? In other words, what were the leader's choices or options?

_____

_____

_____

_____

b)   How do the leader's choices reflect strategic considerations—that is, the anticipated reactions of domestic and international actors? Why do you believe some of the other options were *not* chosen?

_____

_____

_____

_____

_____

Exercise I-3.   *Power, Preferences, and Perceptions*
For each of the international situations below, identify one way in which power, preferences, and perceptions could influence the outcome.

a)   Two countries are negotiating a treaty to reduce trade barriers between themselves.

Power: _____

Preferences: _____

Perceptions: _____

b)   China, Russia, Japan, and the United States negotiate with North Korea over its nuclear weapons and missile testing programs.

Power: _____

Preferences: _____

Perceptions: _____

c) The UN is deciding whether to send an international force into Somalia to end piracy, restore order in the country, and rebuild its government and economy.

Power: _____

Preferences: _____

Perceptions: _____

d) Ethiopia decides whether to attack Eritrea over some disputed territory on their mutual border.

Power: _____

Preferences: _____

Perceptions: _____

CHAPTER 1

THE STRATEGIC PERSPECTIVE

WINNING COALITIONS AND SELECTORATES

Exercise 1-1. *Winning Coalitions and Private Goods*

As you've probably noticed, *Principles* uses a lot of math notation in its explanations. To help you become more comfortable reading and writing in this language, this workbook includes a number of exercises in which you'll have the opportunity to practice translating English into math and math into English. Other times, you'll be manipulating expressions or equations that you created or that come from *Principles*.

For parts a, b, and c, write an expression or equation that says the same thing as the verbal statement. You will want to use some of the following symbols: +, -, *, /, <, ≤, >, and ≥. Please use the variable names indicated in parentheses.

a) The size of the winning coalition (W) can never exceed the size of the selectorate (S), but the two may be equal.

b) A government's revenues (r) are composed of foreign aid (f), natural resource wealth (n), and taxes levied at some rate t ($0 < t < 1$) on all production in the country (y).

c) Consider a situation in which a leader answers to a small winning coalition (w). El Supremo has no need to provide public goods to his people, since his government rests entirely on a small band of cronies (i.e., the members of w). Write an equation to show the amount of private goods (g) that each person gets if the leader distributes all of the country's revenue equally among the winning coalition and himself. (*Hint:* The leader is not part of the winning coalition.)

d) Consider your response to part c of this exercise. For simplicity, let's assume that $r = 10$. If a leader has one member in his w, how much g does each get? Complete Table 1.1 for different values of w and graph your values for $w = 1, 2, \ldots 10$ in the figure. (Leave the column marked g' empty for now.)

TABLE 1.1
Winning Coalition Size and Private Goods

w	g	g'
1		
2		
3		
4		
5		
6		
7		
8		
9		
10		
100		

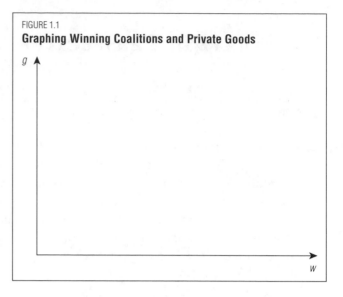

FIGURE 1.1
Graphing Winning Coalitions and Private Goods

e) Based on your graph, what is the effect on *g* of increasing the size of the winning coalition? Why?

_____

_____

_____

f) Consider a situation in which a foreign country makes a donation of foreign aid to El Supremo's state that is worth 2 units. Again, El Supremo has no interest in using this money to provide public goods and intends to distribute it as a private good. What is the new value of *g*—call it *g'*—for this larger pool of revenue? Complete the *g'* (say "g-prime") column in Table 1.1 and add it to your graph in a different color. (Please provide a key for your instructor.)

Exercise 1-2.   *Institutions and Preferences*

For the purposes of this exercise, let's normalize *S* to 1. You can interpret *S*, then, as 100 percent, and *w* as the percentage of people in *S* who are in *w*. (Think of a pie graph in which the whole circle is *S* [*S* = 1] and some shaded area represents *w*.)

a) Write an expression that shows the probability that a member of *S* is also a member of *w*.

b) Write an expression that shows the probability that a member of *S* is *not* a member of *w*.

c) If each member of *w* gets *g* in each period, how much benefit should a member of *S* expect to get in each period? (*Hint:* Review your responses to the previous parts of this question. How much does each member of *w* get, and how likely is she or he to get it?)

Consider that a potential challenger exists, and you, as a member of *w*, are thinking about defecting from the current leader to support the challenger. As a current member of *w*, you get some amount of private goods *g* with certainty (i.e., with probability 1) in the current period and in every future period that you remain a member of *w*. But the challenger has offered you some new amount of private goods, g^*. If you defect and cause the current leader to fall, there is some chance (let's call it *p*) that you'll be a member of *w* in the next period, and you would get g^* from the challenger. There is also some chance, however, that you will *not* be in *w*—perhaps the challenger is unsuccessful or turns on you after entering office—and thus you might get 0 in the next period.

d) Write an expression that shows how much you'd expect to get in the next round if you stay with the current leader.

e) Write an expression that shows how much you'd expect to get if you defect to the challenger in the next period. (*Hint:* What benefit do you get if you are in *w*, and how likely are you to get it? What benefit do you get if you are *not* in *w*, and how likely are you to get it?)

f) How much does the challenger have to offer you to gain your support, relative to what you're getting from the current leader? Would you defect if $g = g^*$? If $g < g^*$? If $g > g^*$? (*Hint:* You want to take the action that maximizes your benefits. Manipulate your responses to the previous two items for this question.)

Let's put the pieces together now.

g) If you are a member of *s* who is not currently in *w*, would you prefer *w* to be larger or smaller? Why? (*Hint:* Think about the pie graph.)

_____

_____

_____

h) If you are a member of *w*, would you support reforms to the government that increased the size of *w*? Why or why not? (*Hint:* Review your work in Exercise 1-1.)

_____

_____

_____

i) If you are a member of *w*, would you prefer that *s* be larger or smaller? Why?

_____

_____

_____

j) Think again about the probability that a member of *s* is in *w* in a future period. If you are the leader, and you believe you will be, at some point in your tenure you will face a challenger. If you want to make your position more secure, what kinds of institutional reforms (i.e., adjustments to the size of *w* or *s*) could you make? Why would these help you retain power?

_____

_____

_____

_____

_____

Exercise 1-3. *The Loyalty Norm*

Let's take a closer look at some of the expressions we wrote above. If you are a member of the current winning coalition, then

$$p\,(g^*) + (1-p)(0) > g \qquad\qquad p = \frac{w}{s}$$

Remember that g is the value of private goods you get from the leader right now, and g^* is some amount of private goods that a potential challenger has offered you if you defect from the current leader. p, the ratio of w to s, tells you how likely you are to be in a new leader's winning coalition, assuming that the size of the selectorate and the size of the winning coalition remain the same from the old leader to the new one.

a) Simplify the two expressions above by substituting the expression for p into the first equation and combining terms.

b) Look at your new expression. Based on your intuition and your work above in Exercises 1-1 and 1-2, what do you think will happen to the left side of the equation as w/s gets smaller? What will have to happen to the value of g^* to make you still prefer the challenger to the current leader—will a low probability of being in the new winning coalition mean that the challenger has to offer you more or less private goods to gain your support?

_____

_____

_____

_____

c) Think about what your expression means. Would you always prefer to take the challenger's offer, g^*? After all, 6 is greater than 5. Why or why not?

_____

_____

_____

Graphing the Relationship

The next several questions ask you to evaluate your expression from part a of this exercise for different values of w and s, and then to graph your results on Figures 1.2 and 1.3. In both figures, assume that g, your private benefit now from the current leader, is equal to 5 units (i.e., $g = 5$). Call your benefit B.

d) Assume for now that $s = 10$ and that $g^* = 6$. For each value of w in Table 1.2, evaluate your expression from part a and note it in the table. (The center column, w/s, is there for your computational convenience.) Graph your results in Figure 1.2 and connect the points with a line.

TABLE 1.2

Evaluating Values of _w_

w	w/s	B
1		
2		
3		
4		
5		
6		
7		
8		
9		
10		

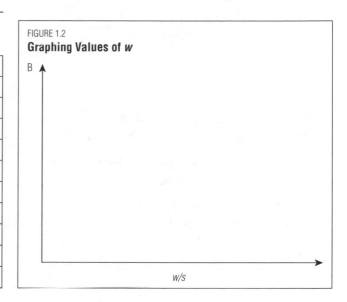

FIGURE 1.2

Graphing Values of _w_

TABLE 1.3

Evaluating Values of _s_

s	w/s	B
1		
2		
3		
4		
5		
6		
7		
8		
9		
10		

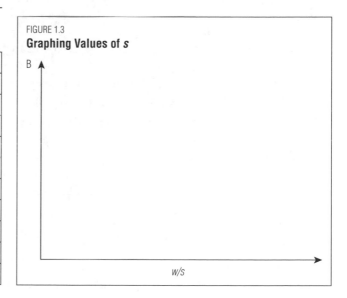

FIGURE 1.3

Graphing Values of _s_

e) Draw a line in Figure 1.2 that represents your current benefits, that is, $g = B = 5$. You may wish to use a different color.

f) Continue to assume that $g^* = 6$. This time, we'll fix $w = 2$. For each value of s in Table 1.3, evaluate your expression from part a and note it in the table. (The center column, w/s, is there for your computational convenience.) Graph your results in Figure 1.3 and connect the points with a line.

g) Draw a line in Figure 1.3 that represents your current benefits, that is, $g = B = 5$. You may wish to use a different color.

h) Consider your graph in Figure 1.2. How sure must you be that you'll be in the new winning coalition—what is the critical value of w/s—that makes you prefer the challenger's offer of $g^* = 6$ over the current leader's $g = 5$? (*Hint:* Think about the two lines you graphed.) Is this a high value of p, or a relatively low one?

i)   Consider your graph in Figure 1.3. How sure must you be that you'll be in the new winning coalition—what is the critical value of w/s—that makes you prefer the challenger's offer of $g^* = 6$ over the current leader's $g = 5$? Is this a high value of p, or a relatively low one?

j)   Think about your responses to the previous two questions. Are you willing to join the challenger at very low levels of p? Why do you think this is true? (*Hint:* Think about the values of g and g^*.)

_____

_____

k)   Imagine that p is very low—say, 0.1. Under these conditions, how much does the challenger have to offer you—what is the critical value of g^*—to gain your support? (*Hint:* Remember that you are currently getting $g = 5$ from the leader.)

The Leader's Perspective
What does all of this mean for the leader? What if you are the leader of a country in which $w/s = 1/5$ (0.2)?

l)   If $g^* = 6$ and $p = w/s = 0.2$, then how much does a member of w expect to benefit if she or he defects to the challenger? Calculate the expected benefit of defecting. Will she or he defect for these values of g^* and p? Why or why not?

_____

_____

_____

m)   As the leader of the country, you had been paying the members of w $g = 5$ to retain their support. Do you really need to pay them this much if $p = 0.2$? If actors are risk-averse (that is, they prefer a sure thing to a risky thing), how much do you need to pay them—what is the critical value of g—to maintain their support? Explain how you got this answer and why this makes sense.

_____

_____

_____

n)   If you reduce g to its critical value, how much g do you save for each member of w? As leader of a small-w system, what happens to the rest of the revenues that you are no longer distributing to supporters? Why?

_____

_____

_____

CHAPTER 2

TOOLS FOR ANALYZING INTERNATIONAL AFFAIRS

THE MEDIAN VOTER THEOREM

The median voter theorem is a powerful tool to analyze social choice. The simple argument of this theorem is that in a group of voters arrayed along some continuous policy dimension, the median voter holds the critical position that will determine the outcome of decisions. That is, the position of the median voter will be the winning position.

Two critical conditions must hold before we can use the median voter theorem to predict outcomes. Actors must have (or be assumed to have) single-peaked preferences, and we must have a *unidimensional issue area*. The median voter theorem only works when we consider issues one at a time.

Exercise 2-1. *The Power of the Median Voter*

Why is the median voter in such a powerful position? Explain, either intuitively or using one or more numerical examples to demonstrate.

_____

_____

_____

_____

Single-peaked Preferences

The strategic perspective normally assumes single-peaked preferences in spatial models. Briefly, an actor with *single-peaked preferences* has one most preferred outcome on a given issue or dimension, and outcomes other than the ideal point give decreasing utility (are less valuable to the actor) as each outcome becomes more distant from the ideal point.

As a practical example, most of us have single-peaked preferences over the amount of sugar in our coffee (or tea). Suzy has an ideal point of three spoonfuls of sugar in a cup of coffee. This point makes her happiest. If she has single-peaked preferences and an ideal point of three spoonfuls, then no amount of sugar gives her greater utility than three spoonfuls. Her utility function (a line or curve showing how an actor's utility changes over different values of variables) peaks at three and, with an assumption of single-peaked preferences, decreases on either side of three without rising again. If for whatever reason Suzy couldn't have 3 spoonfuls of sugar, she would be equally happy with 2.5 spoonfuls *or* with 3.5 spoonfuls, since these are equally distant from her ideal point. As a general rule, actors with single-peaked preferences prefer points closer to their ideal point to those farther away from it, so 2.5 spoons is preferred to 5 spoons, since 2.5 is nearer to the ideal point than 5 is. (Examine Figure 2.1 to verify that these relationships hold and to familiarize yourself with how this works.)

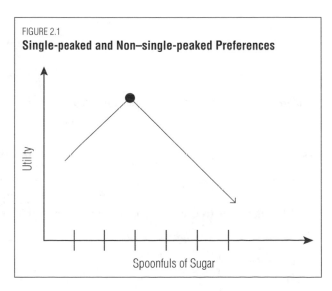

FIGURE 2.1
Single-peaked and Non–single-peaked Preferences

Utility

Spoonfuls of Sugar

In contrast, non–single-peaked preferences have a utility function that reaches a peak at the ideal point and declines, but then turns back upward. This implies that the actor's utility does not continue to decline as he or she moves away from the ideal point—on the contrary, at that bottom point the utility starts to increase again, even though the distance from the ideal point is increasing. If Suzy can't have 3 spoonfuls, she'd next prefer 2 or 4 spoonfuls, but if she couldn't have 2 or 4 she'd rather have 6 spoonfuls. This just doesn't make sense.

Exercise 2-2.   *Single-peaked Preferences*

a)   Draw the non–single-peaked utility function just described on Figure 2.1. (*Hint:* Think about what "to like something more" means in terms of the axes of Figure 2.1.)

b)   Also on Figure 2.1, draw the utility function for an actor whose ideal point is 0 (zero) spoons of sugar. (Please use a dashed line or a different color.) Is this utility function single-peaked? Defend your answer.

_____

_____

_____

The Median Voter Theorem in International Affairs

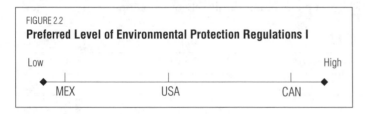

FIGURE 2.2
Preferred Level of Environmental Protection Regulations I

Low   High

　　　MEX　　　　　　　USA　　　　　　　CAN

Exercise 2-3.   *The North American Free Trade Agreement*

It's early 1992, and the United States (USA), Mexico (MEX), and Canada (CAN) are wrapping up negotiations on the North American Free Trade Agreement (NAFTA).

Environmental Standards I

Environmental regulation is costly to business, and it may undercut Mexico's comparative advantage in cheap labor. Canadians, on the other hand, care strongly about the environment. Under Republican president George H. W. Bush (Bush senior), the United States is less concerned about environmental protection than under some previous administrations.

a)   Consider the scenario modeled in Figure 2.2. Using the median voter theorem, what is the outcome of this international negotiating situation? Which actor's ideal point is selected? Why?

_____

_____

_____

_____

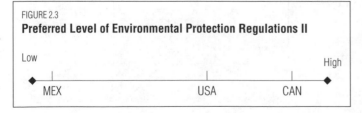

FIGURE 2.3
Preferred Level of Environmental Protection Regulations II

Low   High

　　　MEX　　　　　　　USA　　　CAN

Environmental Standards II

It's now early 1993. The November 1992 U.S. presidential elections produced a rather unexpected upset of a sitting president, bringing Democrat Bill Clinton to the Oval Office with the support of a left-wing coalition of environmentalists, labor, and feminists.

b)   What happens to the U.S. position on labor standards as a result of this change in leadership?

_____

_____

c) Consider Figure 2.3. Using the median voter theorem, which actor's ideal point is selected? What happens to the outcome of this situation, compared to the model in Figure 2.2?

_____

_____

_____

Labor Standards

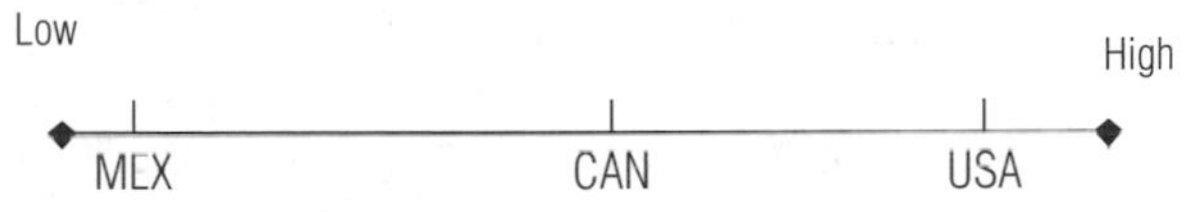

A number of U.S. actors, especially U.S. labor unions, were very concerned about the low level of labor standards (and particularly the very low wages) in Mexico. They feared that this cheap labor pool would cause many jobs to drain from the United States to Mexico—a "giant sucking sound," as third-party conservative candidate Ross Perot described it. After Clinton is elected with the support of many traditional Democratic constituencies, including labor unions, adding labor standards to NAFTA becomes a significant objective.

FIGURE 2.4
Preferred Level of Labor Standards

Low | | High
MEX | CAN | USA

d) Consider Figure 2.4. Using the median voter theorem, what level of labor standards will be agreed on by the parties? How reasonable does this sound given what we know of the interests of the parties?

_____

_____

_____

Weighting the Votes

Let's think about this situation again. All the actors in this situation may be individual sovereign states, but they are not equally powerful. Instead, let's assume that states' votes are weighted by their power. In other words, more powerful actors have more "votes" to cast on a given issue. Look at Figures 2.2 and 2.3 again, but this time allocate 5 votes to Mexico, 10 votes to Canada, and 16 votes to the United States.

e) What is the median vote under these voting weights (how many votes are needed to win)? _____

f) In Figure 2.3, who holds the median (weighted) vote? Is this actor the median voter? What happens to the outcome from part c of this exercise?

_____

_____

_____

g) Using the same distribution of votes, look at Figure 2.4 again. Who holds the median (weighted) vote? Is this actor the median voter? What happens to the outcome from part d of this exercise?

_____

_____

_____

h) What does this result suggest about why powerful countries usually get their way in bilateral or even multilateral international negotiations?

_____

_____

_____

i) *Challenge:* Devise a realistic distribution of votes in which the weighted voting outcome—the ideal point of the holder of the median vote—is the same as the ideal point of the median voter.

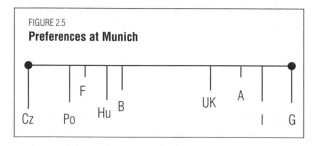

FIGURE 2.5
Preferences at Munich

Exercise 2-4. *Preferences at Munich*

The median voter model in Figure 2.5 depicts the situation at the Munich conference of 1938, when British prime minister Neville Chamberlain and his French and Italian counterparts had to decide what percentage of Hitler's demands for Czechoslovak territory to grant. The actors are Hungary (Hu), the United Kingdom (UK), France (F), Italy (I), Germany (G), Czechoslovakia (Cz), Belgium (B), Austria (A), and Poland (Po).

a) If all actors in the model have one vote, who is the median voter? Is this actor's ideal point a plausible outcome for this situation? Why or why not?

_____

_____

_____

b) If "voting" in this situation is weighted by power, so that more powerful actors have more influence on the outcome, in which direction is the median vote likely to shift? Why?

_____

_____

c) The following voting weights for the actors in the model were developed using the Correlates of War Project's Composite Index of National Capabilities, representing each state's share of capabilities among these actors in 1938. Assuming these weights, which total 100 "votes," where would the outcome be? Is this more plausible than the answer to part b of this exercise? Why or why not?

Cz = 4	Hu = 2	A = 2
Po = 7	B = 3	I = 10
F = 13	UK = 21	G = 38

_____

_____

_____

d) If possible, use your library's resources to obtain and read the cover story of the *New York Times* or the *Washington Post* from September 30, 1938. (If that's not possible, do a bit of research into Hitler's demands and the outcome of the Munich conference.) About where on the issue dimension did the true outcome fall? Does this agree with your model?

_____

_____

_____

_____

SPATIAL MODELING

Spatial modeling is a tool used to analyze behavior when actors have single-peaked preferences over two (or more) linked issues. (More than two issues is possible but more complicated; ask your instructor if you're curious.) Constructing a spatial model requires several pieces of information:

Information about the issues:

- the choices, or options, arrayed on a separate scale for each issue, and
- the location of the *status quo,* or current outcome, for each issue.

Information about the actors:

- the *ideal point,* or most preferred outcome, for each relevant actor on each issue, and
- the nature of each possible *winning coalition,* a set of actors who are able to change the status quo if they agree on a new solution.

As in the median voter theorem, we assume that preferences are single-peaked and that we can conceptualize the issues as single dimensions on which we can rank policy options.

Circular Indifference Curves

Chapter 2 introduced circular indifference curves. An *indifference curve* shows all the points with equal utility to the actor, that is, all the points among which the actor is indifferent. As we discussed earlier, in a spatial model (or any model assuming single-peaked preferences), increasing distance from the ideal point reflects decreases in utility. When actors have single-peaked preferences over two issues (and assuming that the actor cares equally about both issues), we find the set of points that have equal utility to the actor at an equal distance from the actor's ideal point. In two dimensions, this means that the indifference curves are circular, since all the points on a circle are equidistant from its center.

If we assume that the center point represents an actor's ideal point, then that actor will be indifferent to points above, below, or to the side of that preferred position, as long as those alternatives are equidistant from the ideal point. Points on the inside of any indifference curve are more preferred to points outside the curve because they are closer to the ideal point, and points outside the curve are less preferred than points on (or inside) the curve.

Circular indifference curves that pass through the status quo have a special property that makes them particularly useful for our purposes. When a curve is centered on an actor's ideal point and passes through the status quo, the curve describes the set of points that are of equal utility to the actor as the status quo. The assumption of single-peaked preferences implies that any point inside this curve is *better* for the actor than the status quo is, and so the actor would prefer that point to the status quo. Since we are looking for points that actors would accept over the status quo, this useful property of indifference curves that are tangent to the status quo makes these curves the only ones we usually draw.

If we draw these curves for several actors and find that the curves overlap, the actors whose curves overlap prefer any points inside that overlap area to the status quo or any other points outside the curves. A *win set* is an area where these special indifference curves overlap for a *winning coalition,* a group of actors who are sufficiently influential on the issues to be able to change the status quo.

Constructing a Spatial Model

When we construct a spatial model, we make two important assumptions: The actors have single-peaked preferences, and the issues are arranged so that their options represent increasing levels on some scale. For example, in Figure 2.5 in *Principles,* the issues are laid out so that moving right indicates an increasingly militarized nuclear policy and moving upward indicates a foreign response that uses rewards more than punishment. To construct a spatial model:

1. Identify the two linked issues. Draw a *separate* horizontal axis for each, taking care to describe the axes in terms of some increasing value. Each axis represents a unidimensional issue space, a graphical representation of a single issue.

2. Identify the actors' ideal points and the status quo for each issue, and locate these points on your issue axes.

3. Link your issues by turning one vertical, carefully matching the low ends of the individual axes. (The easiest way to do this is to trace one through a sheet of paper and then rotate the paper and trace or copy it into the new location.) Then, locate each actor's ideal point and the status quo in your new multidimensional issue space by following each from its point on the axis out into the center.

4. Construct circular indifference curves for each actor, where the curve centers on the actor's ideal point and is tangent to (passes through) the status quo.

5. Examine your model to locate any areas of overlap, and determine if those areas are win sets.

Exercise 2-5. *NAFTA II*

Exercise 2-3 asked you to consider the various issue areas of the NAFTA agreement separately. Now we consider them jointly in a single spatial model.

a) Figure 2.6 summarizes the information on actor preferences for environmental and labor standards in the NAFTA agreement. Transfer the ideal points and status quo from Figure 2.6 onto Figure 2.7 and locate these points in the new multidimensional space you've created. (*Hint:* Be sure to match the "low" ends of each scale at the origin.)

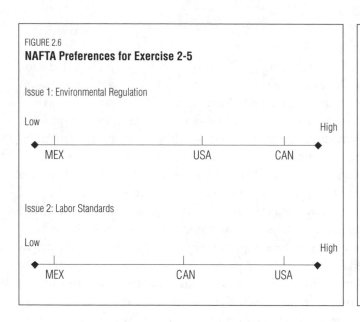

FIGURE 2.6
NAFTA Preferences for Exercise 2-5

Issue 1: Environmental Regulation

Issue 2: Labor Standards

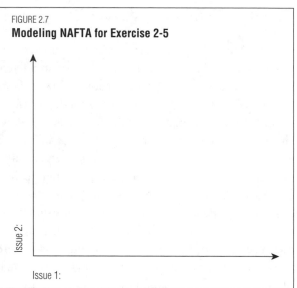

FIGURE 2.7
Modeling NAFTA for Exercise 2-5

b) Because no prior agreement exists on these issues, the status quo is at the "low" endpoint of each axis. Draw circular indifference curves for each actor. Center the curve on the actor's ideal point, and make the radius equal to the distance from the ideal point to the status quo. (*Hint:* You may wish to use a different color for each actor to help you interpret the model.)

c) Assume unweighted voting and majority rule. Under these rules, what win sets exist in your model? Shade or otherwise indicate the win sets in your model. Which win set is most likely to contain the outcome, and why?

d) Consider all the possible two-actor win sets that you found in part c of this exercise. Who is the median voter on each axis? (Assume unweighted voting.) Is this actor the same across both issue dimensions? Is the median actor(s) part of all the possible winning coalitions, or can the other two parties reach an agreement without the median actor's participation? Describe the win sets that do not involve the median actor(s) below, and indicate them on the figure with an asterisk.

_____

_____

_____

_____

e) Assume now that unanimous voting rules apply. Are there any win sets that satisfy all three actors? Discuss why or why not.

_____

_____

_____

Exercise 2-6. *The Doha Development Round*

The Doha Development Round of World Trade Organization (WTO) talks began in Doha, Qatar, in November 2001. Since then, negotiations have bogged down over two related issues: the level of protectionism in the developing world and the level of agricultural subsidies in the developed world. Less-developed countries prefer high levels of protection, particularly on manufactured products and technology, to protect their domestic producers who cannot compete effectively with the highly efficient producers of the developed world. On the other hand, firms in developed countries benefit from lower protection since this enhances their export prospects. Of course, there is some variation among both of these groups, based on characteristics of the economy.

Agricultural protection is a politically salient issue in many developed countries. This is particularly true in the European Union, in which agricultural subsidies consume an enormous (although shrinking) portion of the budget, and in the United States. Government agricultural subsidies enable producers to sell at a lower price than the cost of production, so products are cheaper and more competitive with goods produced in countries with lower costs of production. The ideal points of a select set of WTO members are shown in Figure 2.8. Use this information to construct a spatial model in Figure 2.9.

a) Transfer the ideal points and status quo from Figure 2.8 onto Figure 2.9 and locate these points in the new multidimensional space you've created. (*Hint:* Be sure to match the "low" ends of each scale at the origin.)

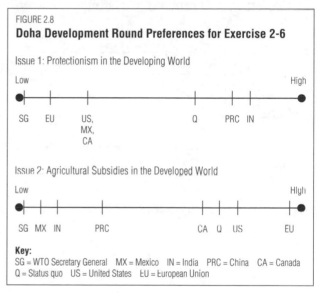

FIGURE 2.8
Doha Development Round Preferences for Exercise 2-6

Issue 1: Protectionism in the Developing World

Low ────────────────────────────── High
SG   EU   US,   Q   PRC IN
          MX,
          CA

Issue 2: Agricultural Subsidies in the Developed World

Low ────────────────────────────── High
SG MX IN   PRC   CA Q US   EU

Key:
SG = WTO Secretary General   MX = Mexico   IN = India   PRC = China   CA = Canada
Q = Status quo   US = United States   EU = European Union

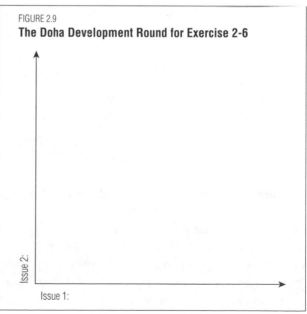

FIGURE 2.9
The Doha Development Round for Exercise 2-6

Issue 2:

Issue 1:

b) Draw circular indifference curves for each actor. Center the curve on the actor's ideal point, and make the radius equal to the distance from the ideal point to the status quo. (*Hint:* You may wish to use a different color for each actor to help you interpret the model.)

c) Several winning coalitions are possible. The United States and EU must be included in any winning coalition. Possible winning coalitions include: Unites States, EU, Canada, and China; and United States, EU, Canada, India, and Mexico. Identify the win sets, if any, that correspond to these winning coalitions. Shade them in some color on your model (please include a key). Which of these win sets is most likely to contain the outcome? Why?

_____

_____

_____

d) Based on your model, in which direction is policy most likely to move? Compare the relative positions of the status quo and the most probable outcome(s) on each dimension.

_____

_____

_____

_____

_____

e) What, if any, potential outcomes from these negotiations are acceptable to the WTO secretary general? What role can the WTO secretary general play in these negotiations, and why might he have an incentive to do this?

_____

_____

_____

_____

_____

f) Use the WTO Web site (www.wto.org) or news sources to find the current status of this dispute. If the dispute has been resolved, does the resolution seem to match your prediction? If the dispute has not been resolved, what is the continued cause of delay?

_____

_____

_____

_____

_____

Exercise 2-7. *Domestic Politics and Spatial Modeling: China and Taiwan*

The biggest potential flashpoint in East Asian security is the ongoing dispute between the Republic of China on Taiwan (*T*) and the People's Republic of China (Mainland China, *M*), over their reintegration into a single country under Beijing's control. Simplifying slightly, Taiwanese preferences have historically been to preserve much autonomy (low integration), while at the same time preserving a high level of peace and security in the region. The status quo is only slightly different from Taiwan's preferred outcome; security is a bit lower and the countries are a bit too integrated for the Taiwanese government's taste.

Mainland China's position is much harder to determine. In the absence of a free press, little reliable information on the Chinese Communist Party's (CCP) internal politics escapes. Taiwanese leaders believe that one of three (hypothetically) possible groups of CCP leaders actually dominates policymaking. The first, M_1, is concerned about the party's internal status in the face of a shaky domestic economy and believes that diverting attention to the Taiwan issue could help preserve order at home. This group prefers a high level of integration, even at the cost of very low security in the region, and is willing to make substantial threats toward Taiwan. It may or may not be willing to actually *use* military force, but it is at least willing to threaten regional security.

M_2, on the other hand, is the result of a power struggle within the CCP: a faction closely tied to the People's Liberation Army (PLA) and a faction interested in gaining capitalist-style investment for the ailing economy have allied to influence policy. This group is willing to invade Taiwan, if necessary, to achieve complete reintegration of the societies (and more important, their economies). It prefers high economic integration and a fairly low level of security.

Finally, the politicians of M_3 are entirely concerned with the state of the domestic economy and believe that the party's hegemony may be threatened if it does not make efforts *soon* to reduce unemployment and increase capital stock. To this group, international military adventures would destabilize the society and the economy and should be avoided at all costs; they are hopeful that Taiwan will react positively and relax some of its restrictions on doing business with the mainland. They would prefer higher regional security and also higher levels of economic integration than currently exist.

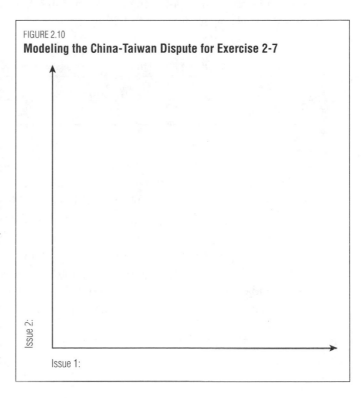

FIGURE 2.10
Modeling the China-Taiwan Dispute for Exercise 2-7

Issue 2:

Issue 1:

a) Construct a spatial model in Figure 2.10 showing the issues in contention, Taiwan, the status quo, and the three possible types of mainland China. Indicate any win sets that may exist. (You may wish to use different colors to clarify your model; if you do, please provide a key.)

b) Is an agreement to change the status quo possible? (*Hint:* What actors constitute a winning coalition here?) With which type(s) of mainland China could Taiwan make an agreement, and which way would the status quo move?

c) Assume that the mainland economy goes into a recession, and party control is threatened. After a major internal leadership struggle and some violence, the faction allied with the PLA (M_2) takes charge. Taiwanese leaders fear that the status quo is unacceptable to these new leaders—that it produces less benefit for them (is too far from their ideal point) than other potential outcomes, which the new mainland leadership might try to take by force.

    While using force to take Taiwan would be costly, the mainland leaders might consider it if they expected large benefits that would substantially exceed the costs. This implies that the mainland's reservation point, its smallest acceptable negotiated outcome, is equal to its costs of taking Taiwan by force. If the mainland leadership's reservation point is closer to the leadership's ideal point than the status quo currently is, is agreement possible? Draw a new indifference curve for M_2 on your model (please use another color) to reflect the new government's reservation point. In most of our other spatial models, what was the outcome if no win set existed? What is the likely outcome here?

_____

_____

_____

_____

d) Taiwan is approaching presidential elections, and the current president's party is unable to field a credible candidate. The first contender, from party A, has categorically refused all integration, even in the face of severe pressure from the mainland; he has vowed to defend the country but will not strike preemptively. Party B's contender, on the other hand, promotes relaxing restrictions on economic interaction with the mainland in an effort to preserve regional peace and security.

    Add A's and B's ideal points to your model. (If your model is already full, please trace it onto another sheet of paper and then do this stage.) Assuming that the status quo represents the minimum acceptable utility for either candidate, is a peaceful settlement possible now between either contender and the mainland? If so, with whom, and in what direction will the status quo shift?

_____

_____

_____

EXPECTED UTILITY

Recall that expected utility is created simply by multiplying the utility of outcomes by the probability that they will actually happen, summing the results over the set of possible outcomes. So, if there are two possible outcomes to a choice, we could write:

$$EU_{choice} = (probability_{outcome\ 1})\ (U_{outcome\ 1}) + (probability_{outcome\ 2})\ (U_{outcome\ 2})$$

More generally,

$$EU_{choice} = (probability_1)\ (U_{outcome\ 1}) + (probability_2)\ (U_{outcome\ 2}) + \ldots + (probability_x)\ (U_{outcome\ x}),$$

where x is the number of possible outcomes.

Exercise 2-8. *Buying a Lottery Ticket I*

A lottery ticket has a lot of utility if you win. But the odds of winning are small, and if you lose, you get nothing. In the first ticket in Table 2.1, the expected utility of the ticket is $0.10. Calculate the expected utility of the second lottery ticket in Table 2.1.

TABLE 2.1

Expected Utility of Two Lottery Tickets for Exercise 2-8

p_{win}	U_{Win}	p_{lose}	U_{lose}	$EU = p_{win}(U_{win}) + p_{lose}(U_{lose})$
.00001	$10000	0.99999	0	0.00001($10000) + 0.99999($0) = $0.10
.001	$2500	0.999	0	

Exercise 2-9. *Starting a War*

Consider what happens if you start a war with another country. Calculate the expected utility in the situations in Table 2.2.

TABLE 2.2

Expected Utility of Different War Situations for Exercise 2-9

	p_{win}	U_{Win}	p_{lose}	U_{lose}	$EU_{war} = p_{win}(U_{win}) + p_{lose}(U_{lose})$
A	0.60	5000	0.40	−5000	0.60(5000) = + 1000
B	0.75	5000	0.25	−5000	
C	0.45	5000	0.55	−5000	
D	0.60	10000	0.40	2000	

Decision Theory

Decision theory is the decision-making model that tells us that given a set of options, or choices, and given an *expected utility* of each option, decision makers will choose the option with the greatest expected utility.

We normally write the condition that given two options, A and B, if $EU_A > EU_B$, the decision maker will choose A. If $EU_A < EU_B$, the decision maker will choose B. If they are equal, the decision maker does not care—that is, he or she is indifferent between the two.

Consider the expected value of the lottery tickets listed in Table 2.1. Based on your odds of winning and the payout, the first ticket had an expected value of ten cents. Let us suppose the ticket cost $1.00. So if you don't buy the ticket you keep $1.00, meaning that the expected value of not buying the ticket is $1.00.

According to decision theory, is it rational to buy the ticket if your utility for money is equal to the quantity of money? The answer is no. Why not? Because $EU_{buy} = \$0.10$, while $EU_{don't\ buy} = \$1.00$.

To review calculating expected utility, see the Walk-Through on the Web site: http://bdm.cqpress.com.

Exercise 2-10. *Buying a Lottery Ticket II*

Based on your odds of winning, the second ticket in Table 2.1 had an expected value of $2.50 (if you calculated correctly). The ticket costs $1.00. Is it rational to buy the ticket? Why or why not?

_____

_____

Exercise 2-11. *The Choice of Where to Go to College*

Before going to college, you made an expected utility calculation about where to send your application, and then once you were admitted, where to choose to attend.

Assume you are deciding to apply to one of three universities: Harvard University, Pennsylvania State University, and East Appalachian State University.

- The utility, or net benefit, of going to Harvard would be great. You would graduate and expect to get a high-paying job, perhaps worth $80,000 or more annually. However, knowing your school record, you might assess the probability that you would 1) be admitted, and 2) graduate with a decent record, to be fairly low—only 30 percent. This implies there is a 70 percent chance you will not complete the degree and be unemployed.
- The utility of going to Penn State is good. Graduates make a good ($40,000) salary on average, and you think it is likely (75 percent) that you will be admitted and will graduate with a good record.
- The utility of East Appalachian State is, unfortunately, not so great. Graduates earn only $20,000 on average. Its advantage is that you are very certain (95 percent) that you will be admitted and will graduate successfully.
- Assume the utility of not going to college, or of going to college and not completing the degree successfully, is 0.

These values are represented in Table 2.3.

TABLE 2.3

Expected Utility of Different Universities for Exercise 2-11

College	Utility (rough, ordinal)	Probability of admission and graduation (rough, ordinal)	Utility (precise, cardinal)	Prob. (precise)	Expected Utility
Harvard	Excellent	Low	80,000	30%	
Penn State	Good	Good	40,000	75%	
E. Appalachian State	Low	Excellent	20,000	95%	

a) Compute the expected utility of each option in Table 2.3 and write it in the table.

b) Which college is the best rational choice in this situation? Why?

_____

_____

Solving for Critical Conditions

Sometimes we want to solve expected utility equations for certain *critical conditions*. By doing this, we find the value of p that is a "tipping point"—the probability of success that makes doing one choice better than another. There are two important steps involved in solving for critical conditions:

- Take the various choices (usually two) that decision maker might make, and set the expected utility of the two equations (choices) equal to each other. (Even if you are given probabilities, don't use them; substitute the variable p instead.)
- Solve algebraically for the condition of interest (usually p). The solution gives the value of the condition at which the decision maker is *indifferent* between the two choices. Given that we know where he or she is indifferent, if the value of the condition changes just a little bit, it will be enough to tip the decision maker one way or the other.

In Exercise 2-11, Penn State was the rational choice of where to attend college. An important question we can answer is, at what point is attempting to attend Harvard rational? That is, what is the critical condition at which $EU_{Harvard}$ becomes greater than $EU_{Penn\ State}$?
To determine this:

- Set the two choices (Harvard and Penn State) equal to each other.

$$EU_{Harvard} = EU_{Penn\ State}$$
$$(P_{get\ into\ Harvard})\,(U_{Harvard}) = (P_{get\ into\ Penn\ State})\,(U_{Penn\ State})$$

- Solve algebraically for the condition of interest. In this case we are interested in learning the critical value of $P_{get\ into\ Harvard}$—that is, how sure we must be that we will successfully graduate (what value p must have)—before we should apply to Harvard. Only one step needs to be done in the algebra, dividing both sides by $U_{Harvard}$.

$$P_{get\ into\ Harvard} = (P_{get\ into\ Penn\ State})\,(U_{Penn\ State})/U_{Harvard}$$

We could now find this value of p numerically. Recall that $U_{Harvard} = 80,000$, $P_{get\ into\ Penn\ State} = 0.75$, and $U_{Penn\ State} = 40,000$. (Since we are solving for $P_{get\ into\ Harvard}$, we do not insert that value from the prior table.) So:

$$P_{get\ into\ Harvard} = (0.75)(40,000)/80,000 = 0.375$$

This critical probability of 0.375 indicates that if you believe your chances of getting into Harvard and graduating are more than 37.5 percent, then applying to Harvard would be better than applying to Penn State.

Exercise 2-12. *Military Attack*

War is an expensive proposition. When considering a military attack, leaders are always uncertain who will win, although they are usually somewhat more certain about what the future holds if they remain at peace. This leads to the following typical situation of deciding what to do in war.

U_{peace} is certain; it is the value of peace, or of the status quo. This is sometimes designated U_{SQ}, or $U_{don't\ attack}$.
EU_{war} is based on risks, so a leader is uncertain how war will turn out because his state might win or might lose. The equation for the expected utility is:

$$EU_{war} = (p_{win})\,(U_{win}) + (p_{lose})\,(U_{lose}).$$

a) How does the equation $EU_{war} = (p_{win})\,(U_{win}) + (p_{lose})\,(U_{lose})$ reflect the description that his state might win or might lose?

_____

_____

b) Say a state has a utility of 100 for peace, and a utility of 500 for winning, but losing is very bad, and so the state has a utility of –1000 for losing. Say the state is equal in strength to the other side, so $p_{win} = 0.5$ and $p_{lose} = 0.5$. Should the state attack? (*Hint:* Compute the expected utilities and compare.) Why?

_____

_____

c) Suppose the utilities are the same as in part b, but that the state has undergone a military buildup. It's now much stronger than the other side, and the military leadership informs the leader that there is a 75 percent chance of winning. All other values are the same as before. Could the state rationally attack now? (*Hint:* Compute the expected utilities and compare.) Why?

_____

_____

Chapter 3

An Introduction to Game Theory

Game Theory: Strategic Form Games

Game theory is the study of decision-making under conditions of strategic interdependence. *Interdependence* means that the players' *payoffs* (values for each outcome) are at least partially conditional on the choices of other actors. The benefit or score or value that you get from breaking your curfew is dependent on the reaction of the people who set the curfew: if you choose to break your curfew and they choose to punish you, this lowers your value for breaking your curfew. *Strategic* actors take the potential actions and reactions of other players into consideration when they choose their own moves. Nonstrategic, or sincere, actors pursue their own best payoff without regard to the potential responses of others. By anticipating others' moves, strategic actors can choose the move that earns them the best available payoff. To continue our example, sincere actors would always break curfew when this could lead to their most preferred outcome. Strategic actors would weigh the possible punishments for breaking curfew into the decision to do it: if the value of staying at the party, less the costs of punishment, is still higher than the value of going home on time, then they would break curfew. If the cost of punishment is much higher than the added gain from staying out later, then these strategic actors would go home.

Constructing a game requires us to know three pieces of information. We must know

1. The players
2. The structure of the game (the moves available to each, as well as the order in which the players move)
3. The players' payoffs for each possible outcome

With these three pieces of information—the players, structure, and payoffs—we can model almost any type of strategic interaction using one of two tools. The choice of which tool we use depends on whether the actors move simultaneously or whether they choose sequentially.

A game in its *strategic, or normal, form* depicts situations in which the actors must move simultaneously, so that neither knows the other's move when he has to choose his own. Alternatively, we can also use this technique to model situations in which the two actors choose without knowing the other's move—for example, in a silent auction, where I write a sealed bid and sometime later you also write a sealed bid. Lack of knowledge on both sides is effectively the same as moving simultaneously. We consider these types of games first. Later in this chapter, we examine *extensive form* games, sometimes called game trees, which depict sequential interaction.

The Prisoners' Dilemma

The Prisoners' Dilemma is the most famous (or at least well-known) example of a strategic form game. The basic dynamics of this game parallel those of a wide range of situations in international relations, from free trade to arms races to environmental protection. In this game, we have two players (we'll colorfully name them A and B). Each player must choose whether to cooperate with the other player—that is, pick move C—or to defect on their agreement by choosing move D. They must make their moves without knowledge of what the other player has chosen, which is to say, the actors move simultaneously, so we use a strategic form game. This represents the first two pieces of information that we need to construct the game: the players (A and B) and the structure of the game (simultaneously, both choose between C and D).

The third piece of information is the players' payoffs for each possible outcome. Two-by-two strategic form games have four possible outcomes, corresponding to the four possible combinations of moves that the players can make. The specific ordering of the payoffs—the ranking of the outcomes—is what makes this game a Prisoners' Dilemma. Many other possible 2×2 games exist with different orderings of payoffs; we'll examine some of those below.

The ordinal payoffs for the Prisoners' Dilemma are shown in Table 3.1. These payoffs match the preferences described in Chapter 3 of *Principles*. In *ordinal payoffs*, different outcomes are rated 4 to 1, reflecting their preference ordering—4 is best (highest payoff), whereas 1 is worst. Recall that every cell contains two values, like (4, 2). These correspond to the payoffs to player A, the row player, followed by the payoffs to player B, the column player.

Given this situation, we can write the players' preference ordering as:

$$DC > CC > DD > CD.$$

This means that the most preferred option for a player is always to defect while the other player cooperates. For player A, this is the lower-left cell of the table. For player B, this is the upper right. The worst option is to cooperate while the other defects. The second-best option is mutual cooperation, and the third-best (second-worst) option is mutual defection. This ordering of payoffs, DC > CC > DD > CD, is what makes this particular game the Prisoners' Dilemma. Using ordinal payoffs, we would write this as:

$$4 > 3 > 2 > 1.$$

In the general terms of the text, we would write these preferences as:

$$\text{Temptation} > \text{Reward} > \text{Punishment} > \text{Sucker.}$$

SOLVING STRATEGIC FORM GAMES

To solve a game, we want to look for the *equilibrium*—that is, a stable prediction of behavior. The most common kind of equilibrium, and the one that we will focus on in this course, is the Nash equilibrium. A *Nash equilibrium* shows a complete set of strategies, one for each player, from which no player would like to defect unilaterally. No player can make himself better off by changing his own move, so neither party has an incentive to choose anything other than his equilibrium strategy.

TABLE 3.1

Prisoners' Dilemma, Player Choices

Player A Choices		B Cooperate	B Defect
A	Cooperate	(3, 3)	(1, 4)
	Defect	(4, 1)	(2, 2)

Player B Choices		B Cooperate	B Defect
A	Cooperate	(3, 3)	(1, 4)
	Defect	(4, 1)	(2, 2)

First, consider what player A will do:

- If A thinks B is going to cooperate: To find this, cover the "B – defect" column with your finger or pencil, then compare A's payoffs in the "B – cooperate" column. If the outcome is CC, A gets 3. But if A defects the outcome becomes DC, and A gets 4. A prefers 4 to 3, so A will defect.
- If A thinks that B is going to defect: To find this, cover the "B – cooperate" column with your finger or pencil, then compare A's payoffs in the "B – defect" column. If the outcome is CD, A gets 1. But if A defects the outcome becomes DD, and A gets 2. A prefers 2 to 1, so A will again defect.
- A thus does better by defecting *no matter what B does*. Defection is a *dominant strategy* for A—it is always best—and so we predict that A will defect.

Now, consider what player B will do:

- If B thinks that A is going to cooperate: To find this, cover the "A – defect" row with your finger or pencil, then compare B's payoffs in the "A – cooperate" row. If the outcome is CC, B gets 3. But if B defects the outcome becomes DC (from B's point of view), and B gets 4. B prefers 4 to 3, so B will defect.

- If B thinks that A is going to defect: To find this, cover the "A – cooperate" row with your finger or pencil, then compare B's payoffs in the "A – defect" row. If the outcome is CD, B gets 1. But if B defects the outcome becomes DD, and B gets 2. B prefers 2 to 1, so B will again defect.

- Like A, B thus does better by defecting *no matter what A does.* Defection is a dominant strategy for B, and we predict that B will also defect.

These decisions are represented in Table 3.1. Arrows represent what each player would do at each cell; underlined values show which payoffs we're comparing. For example, in the top left cell, player A would prefer to defect (move down) because it would get a 4 rather than a 3. At the top left cell, player B would also prefer to defect, hoping that it can get a 4 rather than a 3 also.

Knowing what each player will do, we can put the choices together. We could simply say that because each player has a dominant strategy of defection, they will both defect, and we will obtain DD as an outcome. To write the solution to a strategic form game in equilibrium notation, we simply write the combination of moves—here (D, D)—that results in the equilibrium outcome.

We could also walk through each cell of the game, as in Table 3.2. If we consider the possible outcome to be CC, then both players have an incentive to defect. If the outcome is expected to be that A cooperates while B defects (the upper right cell), then A has an incentive to switch to defection. If the outcome is expected to be that B cooperates while A defects, then B has an incentive to switch to defection. Only at the bottom right cell, mutual defection,

TABLE 3.2

Prisoners' Dilemma, Combined Player Choices, and Nash Equilibrium

A	B Cooperate	Defect
Cooperate	(3, 3)	(1, 4)
Defect	(4, 1)	(2, 2)

does *neither* player want to change moves *on his own.* Once the players reach DD, if either player unilaterally changes his strategy, he loses. DD is thus the Nash equilibrium of a Prisoners' Dilemma game. In this case, "Defect" is a *dominant strategy* for each player in this game. It dominates, or always gives a better payoff, than any other strategy choice available to each player. A player with a dominant strategy will always play that dominant strategy.

But given that DD is the equilibrium, note the dilemma that the players now face which gives this game its name. It is perfectly rational and understandable that the players end up at DD. After all, each has a dominant strategy to defect. But this leads to an outcome with which *both* players are unhappy! The players receive (2, 2), a suboptimal payoff, at DD. By acting individually rationally, the players reach an outcome (DD) that is inferior for both of them. Each could receive a better payoff of (3, 3) if they could get to CC, but there is no reliable way to get there. As soon as one player appears to be cooperating, the other has an incentive to defect. And as soon as one appears to be defecting, the other does not want to be a sucker, and so he also defects. The dilemma is this: cooperation could make both parties better off, but they have no way to enforce it.

MORE REVIEW

The text Web site, http://bdm.cqpress.com, contains a Walk-Through and a handout on solving strategic form games. If you're having trouble determining whose payoffs to compare where, these may be helpful.

Practice Solving Strategic Form Games

Exercise 3-1. *The Prisoners' Dilemma in International Politics*
The Prisoners' Dilemma fits any situation in which:

a) two actors must make simultaneous decisions (or make a decision without knowing what the opponent will do or has done already),

b)   defection always dominates cooperation, and

c)   the preference ordering for *both* players is DC > CC > DD > CD.

We must meet all three conditions to call the game Prisoners' Dilemma; if the first two conditions are met but the preference ordering is different for each player, or the same for both players but different from the one here, it becomes a different strategic form game with different implications (see below). The Prisoners' Dilemma situation, though, intuitively appears very common in international politics—so important that your professor may well ask you to memorize it. Here are two examples.

Arms Control Negotiations

Table 3.3 presents a game that states face when they engage in arms control negotiations. You can think of the players as being the United States and Soviet Union during the cold war, India and Pakistan, Iraq and Iran, or any other two mutually suspicious countries with a history of poor relations.

a)   Go through the cells of the game and think about each outcome. What is the likely preference ordering for state A? For state B? (That is, what outcome does each prefer, and what is the ordering of CC, DD, CD, and DC?)

TABLE 3.3

Prisoners' Dilemma in Arms Control

A	B Cooperate Reduce Arms	B Defect Continue Buildup
Cooperate Reduce Arms	Mutual arms cuts; both sides save money and maintain security	A is vulnerable; B gets military advantage
Defect Continue Buildup	A gets military advantage; B is vulnerable	Arms Race; both sides spend money and gain no security

b)   Write the ordinal preferences (4, 3, 2, 1) for each player in Table 3.3.

c)   What do we expect the outcome of the game to be? Draw in what each player would do in Table 3.3 and solve the game for the equilibrium. Write the equilibrium in equilibrium notation under the game.

d)   Which problem(s) of cooperation—coordination, distribution, monitoring, or sanctioning—does this game show? Briefly explain your response.

Trade

Table 3.4 presents a game that states face when they attempt to make trade agreements. You can think of the players as being the United States and Japan, the United States and China, the United States and the European Community, or any other two countries that say they want to engage in free trade but are concerned that the other side might cheat on the agreement. (An example of such "cheating" occurred in 2003 when the United States defected on its agreement with the WTO by raising tariffs on imported steel.)

e)   Examine the cells of the game and think about each outcome. What is the likely preference ordering for state A? For state B? (That is, what is the ordering of CC, DD, CD, and DC?)

f)   Write the ordinal preferences (4, 3, 2, 1) for each player in Table 3.4.

g)   What do we expect the outcome of the game to be? Draw in what each player would do in Table 3.4 and solve the game for the equilibrium. Write the equilibrium in equilibrium notation under the game.

h)   Which problem(s) of cooperation—coordination, distribution, monitoring, or sanctioning—does this game show? Briefly explain your response.

TABLE 3.4

Prisoners' Dilemma in Trade

| | B | |
A	Cooperate Reduce Tariffs	Defect Impose New Tariffs
Cooperate **Reduce Tariffs**	Increased Free Trade	A loses jobs because of reduced exports from A; B increases revenue from tariffs
Defect **Impose New Tariffs**	B loses jobs because of reduced exports from B; A increases revenue from tariffs	Trade War: exports decrease, jobs lost in both states, tariff revenues decline as trade slows

---

Exercise 3-2. *Other Strategic Form Games in International Politics*

The prisoners' dilemma is just one particular game, which is defined by the preference ordering for each country being DC > CC > DD > CD. But we can represent many situations using 2x2 normal form games. Many of these games take on "cute" names like the prisoners' dilemma, stag hunt, or chicken, but they can also correspond to real-world situations.

There are a few steps involved in analyzing any situation using normal form games such as the prisoners' dilemma:

- What are the choices? What do cooperation and defection correspond to in the real world (for example, building arms vs. not building arms)?
- What are the preferences of leaders or states across DC, DD, CC, and CD? What would a leader prefer and why?
- Lay out the preference orderings as 4 > 3 > 2 > 1 (for example, CD > DD > CC > DC).
- Write the preferences for both sides as payoffs in a 2x2 normal form game. (Assume in these games that both players have the same preference ordering. In real life this is not always true, but in some stylized cases like these it works.)
- Analyze the game for what will happen by looking for one or more equilibria.

Chicken

Say that I am one of two drivers racing down a deserted road and you are the other. We are racing straight toward each other. Our friends are watching us to see who has more guts. I want you to swerve, while I keep going. If you swerve, you are a chicken, and I gain status among our peers. If both of us swerve, then it's an okay outcome, because neither of us gains or loses respect, and we both may gain some respect with everyone else just because we played. If I swerve and you don't, then I am chicken and lose status among our peers; I don't like this much. But if neither of us swerves, we are both dead and it doesn't matter (this is the worst outcome for both of us—better to be a live chicken than a dead duck).

This game was made famous in the 1950s by interactions (including several deaths) between teenaged males in the United States, especially.

The preferences for the game are: DC > CC > CD > DD.

a) Solve the game in Table 3.5 for the Nash equilibrium as we did previously. (*Hint:* There are actually two possible equilibria.) Write the equilibria in equilibrium notation under the game.

TABLE 3.5
Chicken

A	B Cooperate Swerve	Defect Drive Straight
Cooperate Swerve	(3, 3)	(2, 4)
Defect Drive Straight	(4, 2)	(1, 1)

b) Which problem(s) of cooperation—coordination, distribution, monitoring, or sanctioning—does this game show? Briefly explain your response.

_____

_____

_____

c) What situations in international relations might fit this kind of confrontation? Think of a situation (a specific example or a kind of interaction) in which state preferences and interactions might fit those described.

_____

_____

_____

Stag Hunt

Stag Hunt is characterized by a strong interest in cooperation, as long as each actor is certain that the other is cooperating. But if you as a player see that the other side is going to defect for some reason, you would also prefer to defect. The story of stag hunt is that two hunters are hunting a deer in the forest. It requires the cooperation of both hunters to capture the deer, which can feed the entire village. Instead of cooperating, though, the hunters can choose to defect to capture a rabbit, which will feed only one family. Hunters prefer to cooperate and capture the deer, but neither wants to be left waiting for a comrade if he or she runs off to get a rabbit.

The preferences for the game are: CC > DC > DD > CD.

d) Solve the game in Table 3.6 for the Nash equilibrium as we did previously. Write it in equilibrium notation under the game.

TABLE 3.6
Stag Hunt

A	B Cooperate	Defect
Cooperate	(4, 4)	(1, 3)
Defect	(3, 1)	(2, 2)

e) Which problem(s) of cooperation—coordination, distribution, monitoring, or sanctioning—does this game show? Briefly explain your response.

_____

_____

_____

f) What situations in international relations might fit this kind of interaction? Think of a situation in which state preferences and interactions might fit those described.

_____

_____

_____

Deadlock

Occasionally, there may be so many conflicting interests between state leaders that cooperation is absolutely impossible, and leaders do not even want it. Cooperation will never occur in a situation of deadlock, even with repeated interaction.

The preferences for the game are: DC > DD > CC > CD.

g) Solve the game in Table 3.7 for the Nash equilibrium as we did previously. Write it in equilibrium notation under the game.

h) Which problem(s) of cooperation—coordination, distribution, monitoring, or sanctioning—does this game show? Briefly explain your response.

TABLE 3.7

Deadlock

A	B Cooperate	Defect
Cooperate	(2, 2)	(1, 4)
Defect	(4, 1)	(3, 3)

_____
_____
_____

i) What situations in international relations might fit this kind of confrontation? Think of a situation in which state preferences and interactions might fit those described.

_____
_____
_____

Harmony

Occasionally, states or leaders have only very few conflicting interests, and so cooperation is natural, almost a given. In such a situation, you may not care if the other side defects, and in fact you might want to cooperate no matter what it does.

The preferences for the game are: CC > CD > DC > DD.

j) Solve the game in Table 3.8 for the Nash equilibrium as we did previously. Write it in equilibrium notation under the game.

k) Which problem(s) of cooperation—coordination, distribution, monitoring, or sanctioning—does this game show? Briefly explain your response.

TABLE 3.8   _— wrong_   Table 3.9 = Harmony.

Harmony

A	B Cooperate	Defect
Cooperate	(2, 2)	(1, 4)
Defect	(4, 1)	(3, 3)

_____
_____

l) What situations in international relations might fit this kind of interaction? Think of a situation in which state preferences and interactions might fit those described.

_____
_____
_____

Coordination

Often players have multiple solutions to problems of common concern, but they must agree on one solution. As a very basic example, consider driving. Everyone in society benefits from everyone driving on the same side of the road. It really doesn't matter if the norm is to drive on the right (as in the United States) or the left (as in the United Kingdom), as long as everyone agrees. Preferences might be as follows:

The preferences for the game are: CC = DD > DC = CD.

TABLE 3.9
~~Coordination Game~~ *Harmony Game*

A	B Cooperate Left	Defect Right
Cooperate	(4, 4)	(3, 2)
Defect	(2, 3)	(1, 1)

m) Solve the game in Table 3.9 for the Nash equilibria as we did previously. Write it in equilibrium notation under the game.

n) Which problem(s) of cooperation—coordination, distribution, monitoring, or sanctioning—does this game show? Briefly explain your response.

_____

_____

_____

o) What situations in international relations might fit this kind of interaction? Think of situations in which states' preferences and interactions might fit those described.

_____

_____

_____

Exercise 3-3. *Confrontation*

Table 3.10 contains a blank game that you will use to represent a confrontation between two countries for Exercise 3-3.

Assume that the two countries have the following preferences:

■ A (the row player) is a country that will take advantage of other countries if it can. It prefers to defect while other countries cooperate. But, if it can't successfully defect on the other, it prefers mutual cooperation. It least prefers to be a sucker.

■ A's preferences then are DC > CC > DD > CD.

■ B (the column player) is a peace-loving country and prefers mutual cooperation above all else. But if it must defect to get another country to cooperate (by punishing it, for example), then it will—this is its second most preferred outcome. B least prefers to end up in a situation of mutual defection.

■ B's preferences then are CC > DC > CD > DD.

a) Write the payoffs that fit these preferences in Table 3.10.

b) Solve the game you just wrote for the Nash equilibrium or equilibria. Write your answer(s) in equilibrium notation under the game.

TABLE 3.10
Blank Table for Exercise 3-3

A	B Cooperate	Defect
Cooperate		
Defect		

c) Which problem(s) of cooperation—coordination, distribution, monitoring, or sanctioning—does this game show? Briefly explain your response.

_____

_____

_____

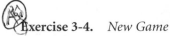

Exercise 3-4. *New Game*

Table 3.11 contains a blank game to use for Exercise 3-4.

Assume that the two players have the following preferences:

- A prefers to take advantage of others if it can. But, if it cannot, it prefers mutual cooperation. For some reason, A wants to avoid mutual defection at all costs (perhaps mutual defection represents a major war). A's next-to-last choice is to give in to B. This is still better than mutual defection.
- A's preferences therefore are DC > CC > CD > DD.
- B prefers mutual cooperation for everyone. But if there is going to be defection, B wants to be the one doing the defecting. B least wants to be a sucker in this situation.
- B's preferences therefore are CC > DC > DD > CD.
  a) Write the payoffs that fit these preferences in Table 3.11.
  b) Solve the game you just wrote for Nash equilibria. Can you tell what will happen in this situation? (*Hint:* the result might be surprising.) Write the equilibrium in equilibrium notation below the game.
  c) Describe the outcome you find in Table 3.11 in words. What is happening here?

TABLE 3.11

Blank Game for Exercise 3-4

A	B	
	Cooperate	Defect
Cooperate		
Defect		

  d) Which problem(s) of cooperation—coordination, distribution, monitoring, or sanctioning—does this game show? Briefly explain your response.

Exercise 3-5. *Hypothetical Confrontation between the United States and China*

Consider the real-world situation of relations between the United States and China over Taiwan. Taiwan has an ambiguous status with respect to independence. Most people in the West, and many in Taiwan, consider Taiwan to be an independent country. Others, including the leadership in China, see Taiwan as a breakaway republic that is actually part of the People's Republic of China. The United States has been an ally of Taiwan but has a strong interest in maintaining and improving relations with mainland China. One interesting question to ask is whether the United States and China would go to war over Taiwan if there were a major crisis. We can analyze this situation using a 2 × 2 game.

Assume that a crisis has begun over the status of Taiwan. China has threatened to attack Taiwan if it does not renounce its claims of independence. The United States, in turn, has threatened to attack China if it attacks Taiwan.

Cooperation in this case involves backing down or offering some kind of concession.

Defection involves escalation of the confrontation by either side—using military forces to attack or refusing to give in—leading to a more dangerous situation.

DD would involve both sides escalating to a war. Trade and peaceful interaction between the United States and China would end.

CC would involve both sides agreeing to negotiate, leading to a peaceful resolution of the crisis with the status of Taiwan still unresolved. Trade and peaceful interaction between the United States and China would continue.

DC would involve the first state escalating while the other backed down, ending the crisis short of war but giving an advantage to the first state.

CD is just the opposite, with the first state backing down while the second escalated the conflict, ending the crisis short of war but giving an advantage to the second state.

a) Speculate about U.S. and Chinese preferences across the four outcomes. What is the preference ordering for each side? That is, think about whether the United States would prefer CC > DD > CD > DC, or DD > DC > CD > CC, or something else, and why. Then, think about what preference ordering China would have. Briefly justify your choice of preference orderings: Why would the state want the outcomes in that particular order?

U.S.:

China:

_____

_____

_____

_____

b) Label the game in Table 3.12 for the two actors, the United States and China. Decide which actor plays the rows and which the columns, and establish what actions "cooperate" and "defect" mean in this situation.

TABLE 3.12

United States and China Confrontation

A	B	
	Cooperate	Defect
Cooperate		
Defect		

c) Write the ordinal payoffs that fit the preference orderings in part a in Table 3.12.

d) Solve the game in Table 3.12 for any Nash equilibria, and indicate it below the game in equilibrium notation.

e) Describe the equilibrium your actors reach (or the equilibria between which they must choose). Does this seem reasonable given your intuition about the real-world situation?

_____

_____

_____

GAME THEORY: EXTENSIVE FORM GAMES

As we discussed above, we use extensive form games to depict and analyze situations in which the actors move sequentially. To analyze a situation in which players are making sequential interactive decisions, we must do the following:

1. Write the game.
    - Draw the tree (extensive) form, with branches that represent options or choices.
    - Label the *decision nodes,* in which actors make decisions, with the actors' names.
    - Label the *outcome,* or *terminal,* nodes.
    - Write in the *payoffs.* By convention, the first mover's payoffs are usually written first, followed by other actors in the order that they move.[1]

Take a moment to examine Figure 3.1 and identify these components of a game.

2. Solve the game using *backwards induction.*
    - Starting on the right side of the tree, calculate—at each decision node where there are options—which option is more preferred for the actor making the decision. Do this by comparing that actor's payoffs from each of his or her available choices. Highlight the branch that is selected.
    - Continue to work toward the left. If you ever encounter a decision node where it is unclear what will happen on the right, go down the tree to the right until you reach a spot where there is a clear decision and work back.

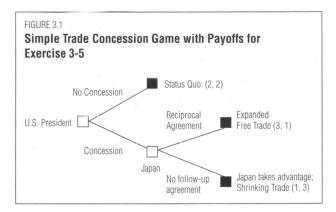

FIGURE 3.1

Simple Trade Concession Game with Payoffs for Exercise 3-5

From the first decision in the game, follow the choices that you highlighted as being selected at each decision until you reach a terminal node. That highlighted terminal node at the end of the equilibrium path is the expected outcome. This continuous string of selected moves is the *equilibrium path,* or expected set of behaviors. The complete equilibrium, however, includes both the combination of strategy choices each player would make—on and off the equilibrium path. Why do moves off the equilibrium path matter? They matter because the *anticipation* that players would make those moves caused other players to alter their own behavior at earlier points in the game. Do not ever scratch out branches that are not selected (i.e., ones that are "pruned")—you will frequently need to refer to those branches later. For simple games, it may not seem like a big deal, but our games will get much more complex very quickly, so get into a good habit now.

You probably noticed as you did backwards induction that the reasoning of backwards induction sounds an awful lot like the reasoning we used above to find Nash equilibria—"If the other player is going to pick A, which move makes me better off?" We've simply extended that kind of reasoning to include a sequential component—"If he will respond to my move A by doing C, and he will respond to my move B by doing D, which move gets me a better outcome, A or B?" If a rational actor knows all of the choices available to other players, knows the order in which players move, and knows everyone's payoffs at all of the outcomes, she can predict others' future moves and judge her own moves based on the expected reactions of others. The form of equilibria that we use in sequential games is a refinement of the basic Nash equilibrium concept we used earlier. It is called a *subgame perfect equilibrium.*[2]

---

[1] For now, we'll assume that all of the players know all of the previous moves (that is, that they have perfect information), and that they all know each others' preference orderings (that is, they have complete information). These are only assumptions, however, and we can relax them if doing so provides a better model of a situation. In this book, we will always assume complete and perfect information; if you're curious, more advanced texts on game theory (or your instructor) can show you how to solve games where information is incomplete or imperfect.

[2] Officially, a subgame perfect equilibrium requires that at each point where an actor makes a choice, his choice is the best response to the expected responses of others to that move. Our original Nash definition requires best responses, but notice that this new definition expands it to include each point at which an actor makes a decision, and by extension, it requires that each player is playing his Nash best response strategy at every subgame.

In a subgame perfect equilibrium, we must expand our definition of what constitutes a "strategy" for an actor to play. In a strategic form game, actors only make one choice; their possible strategies are simply the sets of moves available to them in that game. In an extensive form game, a *strategy* is a complete set of moves for an actor, one for each of the actor's choice nodes, so that the actor knows what move to play no matter at what node he finds himself.

Writing equilibria is easy for strategic form games because each player only moves once. When we write out a complete subgame perfect equilibrium, we must always include these off-path moves. A common format to write equilibria for extensive form games is to list player 1's moves then player 2's moves, with each player's moves separated with a comma and the players themselves separated with a semicolon.

(Player 1: move at node 1, move at node 3, etc.; Player 2: move at node 2, move at node 4, etc.)

We do not distinguish here between moves on and off the equilibrium path. If your game is fairly complex, you may want to number your choice nodes so that readers can follow your notation. We would normally number top to bottom for vertical trees (left to right for horizontal trees) for each successive stage of the game (layer of nodes).

This is not the only way to write equilibria, but you should use it until your instructor shows you an alterative that he or she prefers. It is generally *not* accepted, however, to write equilibria by simply starting at the beginning of the game and listing each move in order regardless of who makes it. As we discussed above, a strategy is a complete set of moves for all contingencies for a single player, so we want to report our findings—our equilibria—in a way that shows a complete strategy for each player.

Also, you may choose to abbreviate "not" in your games and equilibria with the symbol "~."

Solving Games with Backwards Induction

Figure 3.1 on the previous page presented a game between the United States and Japan over trade.

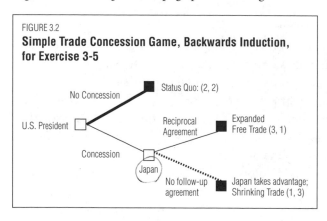

FIGURE 3.2

Simple Trade Concession Game, Backwards Induction, for Exercise 3-5

Preferences for the United States: The United States prefers expanded free trade to the status quo and prefers the status quo to shrinking trade, which results from Japan taking advantage of the United States.

So for the United States: Expanded Free Trade > Status Quo > Japanese Advantage.

Preferences for Japan: Japan prefers to take advantage of U.S. concessions. Japan's second best option is the status quo, and its least preferred option is expanded trade.

So for Japan: Japanese Advantage > Status Quo > Expanded Free Trade.

As before, this game uses ordinal payoffs that simply represent the order in which the actor prefers the choices. Actors always prefer larger values over smaller ones. Figure 3.2 contains the backwards induction solution to the game.

■ Start at the Japan decision node, *as far down the tree to the right as possible*. Which option does Japan prefer? Japan prefers to take advantage of the United States at this point (Japan receives a payoff of 3, which is better than 1). Note that Japan will consider *only* its own payoffs—it does not care about U.S. payoffs.[3]

■ We mark Japan's choice in Figure 3.2 by a heavier dotted line. This indicates the path that Japan will take from its final decision point.

■ Move left to the U.S. decision node. The United States now knows that if it moves to offer a concession, Japan will not reciprocate. It will choose to take advantage of the U.S. concession, leaving the United States with a payoff of 1. The United States then has the choice between a 1 if it offers a concession and a 2 if it does not. Since the United States prefers 2 to 1, it will choose not to offer a concession.

---

[3]If Japan did care, we would rewrite the payoffs; we assume that the payoffs written on a game take into account all the players' considerations about what happens.

- We mark the U.S. decision with a heavy line in Figure 3.2 to indicate its decision.
- The outcome that we expect in this game is the status quo. <u>The complete equilibrium here is "no concession;</u> <u>no follow-up agreement."</u> Notice that even though Japan does not get to move in this equilibrium, the *expectation* of how Japan would respond causes the United States to change its behavior from the pursuit of its sincere top preference—expanded free trade—to an acceptance of the continued status quo.

Exercise 3-6. *Solving Extensive Form Games by Backwards Induction*

The games below depict a wide range of situations using extensive form games. Solve each using backwards induction, according to the prompts. Always show your work on the figures by highlighting or darkening the selected line. Never cross out "pruned" branches—you will need them later!

United States–Japanese Trade, New Japanese Government

A new Japanese government comes to power. It prefers no change in world trade, but does not want to take advantage of the United States. So, its preferences are Status Quo > Expanded Free Trade > Japanese Advantage. U.S. preferences remain the same.

a) Write the new preferences in the game in Figure 3.3.

b) Solve the game by backwards induction. Show your work by marking the figure.

c) Write out the full equilibrium for the game.

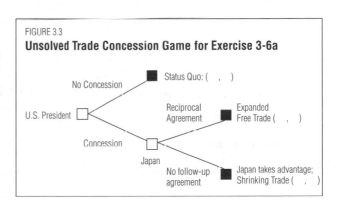

FIGURE 3.3
Unsolved Trade Concession Game for Exercise 3-6a

A Generic Game

The game in Figure 3.4 does not use ordinal payoffs (4, 3, 2, 1) but instead uses actual cardinal utility values (200, 400, etc.). Higher values are still preferred to lower values. (Game adapted from James Morrow, *Game Theory for Political Scientists* [Princeton: Princeton University Press, 1994].)

d) Solve this game by backwards induction, making sure to show your work by marking the tree. The game is more complicated than previous ones, but the same principles of how to solve it apply. (*Hint:* Remember in what order payoffs are written.)

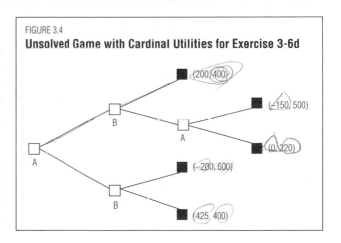

FIGURE 3.4
Unsolved Game with Cardinal Utilities for Exercise 3-6d

Exercise 3-7. *Presidential and Congressional Legislation*

The exercise below asks you to consider two different scenarios of presidential and congressional preferences over a piece of legislation. Use ordinal payoffs to help construct each game.

Presidential and Congressional Legislation I

The president must decide whether to design a bill that has in it only minor reforms or one that represents a major overhaul of the current system. Once the president's supporters offer the bill, the full Congress can either accept or reject the legislation. Of course, both the president and members of Congress have an interest in good legislation and in scoring political points.

Outcomes:

- If a minor bill is offered by the president's supporters and enacted by Congress, then some minor reform will occur.
- If a minor bill is offered, but Congress rejects it, there is no reform and the public reacts angrily against a "do-nothing" Congress that is unwilling to take even minor steps to improve the country.
- If a major bill is offered and enacted, the president receives a popularity boost and becomes known as someone who can get things done. But Congress does not want the president to become more popular and so is unhappy with this option.
- If a major bill is offered but is rejected by Congress, no reform occurs, and the president is hurt because his or her favorite initiative was defeated. But because the bill was so major, many in the United States are suspicious of it, and public opinion is mixed over the defeat. A Congress opposed to the president likes this outcome, because it can claim that it turned back radical proposals that would have destabilized the country.

Preferences:

- President: Major initiative enacted > minor reforms enacted > rejected minor bill > rejected major bill.
- Congress: Rejected major bill > minor reforms enacted > rejected minor bill > major initiative enacted.

a) Write the preferences in the game in Figure 3.5. Use ordinal preferences.

b) Solve the game by backwards induction. Show your work in the figure.

c) Write out the full equilibrium of the game.

FIGURE 3.5
Unsolved Reform Game for Exercise 3-7a

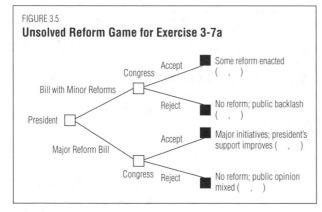

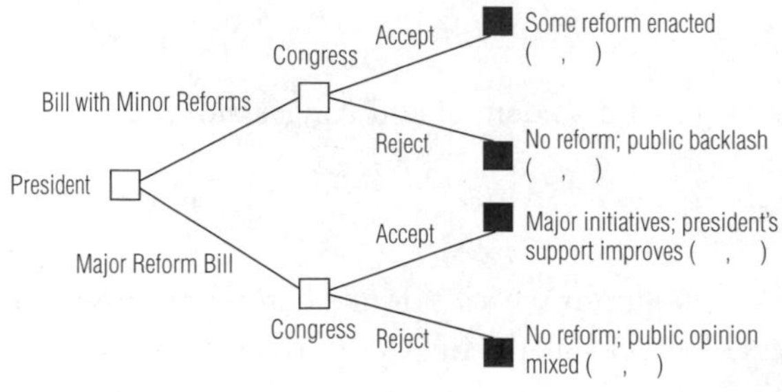

Presidential and Congressional Legislation II

What if the president wants to portray Congress as "do nothing" no matter what? In this case the president prefers to have Congress reject a major bill, then reject a minor bill, then accept major initiatives, then accept minor initiatives. Congress's preferences remain the same. So:

- President: Rejected minor bill > rejected major bill > major initiative enacted > minor reforms enacted.
- Congress: Rejected major bill > minor reforms enacted > rejected minor bill > major initiative enacted.

d) Write the preferences in the game in Figure 3.6. Use ordinal preferences.

e) Solve the game by backwards induction. Show your work in the figure.

f) Write out the full equilibrium of the game.

FIGURE 3.6
Unsolved Reform Game for Exercise 3-7d

President — Bill with Minor Reforms — Congress — Accept — Some reform enacted (,)
— Reject — No reform; public backlash (,)
Major Reform Bill — Congress — Accept — Major initiatives; president's support improves (,)
— Reject — No reform; public opinion mixed (,)

Exercise 3-8. *Arms Control*

Countries often must decide whether to take a first step in starting arms control negotiations by offering a major cut to the other side. The problem is (as with trade) that the other country might reciprocate or might take advantage of the gesture. If the other side continues to build weapons when the first nation makes major cuts, it will achieve a potentially significant military advantage.

- Soviet Union: Major Soviet Union advantage > Slight Soviet Union advantage = Significant arms reduction > Slight U.S. advantage.
- United States: Significant arms reduction > Slight U.S. advantage > Slight Soviet Union advantage > Major Soviet Union advantage.

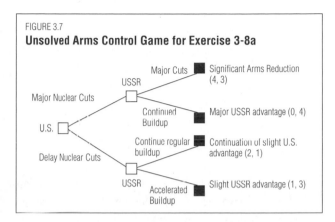

FIGURE 3.7
Unsolved Arms Control Game for Exercise 3-8a

a) The payoffs in this game (Figure 3.7) are written with values other than the 1, 2, 3, 4 of prior games. Verify that the numbers used here are still ordinal and still reflect the preference orderings given.

b) Solve the game by backwards induction. Show your work on the figure.

c) Think about what makes the two sides make their respective choices. Devise a modified preference ordering for the Soviet Union that would result in the two sides agreeing to significant mutual arms reduction. (Note: There may be more than one preference ordering that will achieve this.)

Soviet Union preference ordering:

_____

_____   _____

d) Are these payoffs you posited realistic? Why or why not?

_____

_____

_____

_____

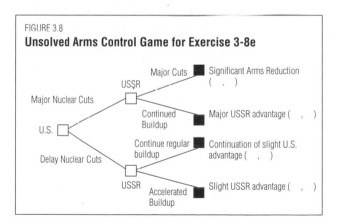

FIGURE 3.8
Unsolved Arms Control Game for Exercise 3-8e

e) Write your new preference ordering for the Soviet Union and the original U.S. preference ordering of the two sides in the game tree in Figure 3.8, using ordinal preferences. Then show the backwards induction solution to the game you have created in Figure 3.8.

Arms Control II

The United States has developed new technology that will allow it to detect if the Soviet Union is not backing off its buildup. This gives the United States another final move during which it can decide to accelerate its arms production over the Soviet Union, resulting in a much greater U.S. advantage than before (this is equivalent to the United States getting mad and responding forcefully to the Soviet betrayal of its promised nuclear cuts). The United States would prefer to have significant arms reductions, but if it cannot have that, the United States would rather have as large an advantage as possible.

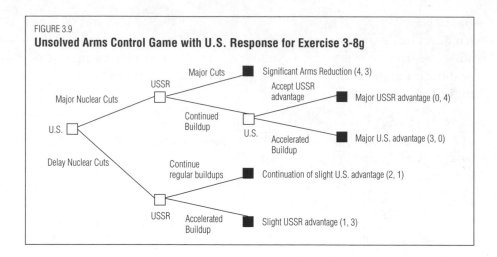

FIGURE 3.9
Unsolved Arms Control Game with U.S. Response for Exercise 3-8g

- United States: Significant arms reduction > Major U.S. advantage > Slight U.S. advantage = Slight Soviet Union advantage > Major Soviet Union advantage.
- Soviet Union: Major Soviet Union advantage > Slight Soviet Union advantage = Significant arms reduction > Slight U.S. advantage > Major U.S. advantage.

f) Verify for yourself that the preference orderings written in the game satisfy the listed preference orderings.

g) Solve the game in Figure 3.9 by backwards induction. Show your work in the figure.

h) Write out the full equilibrium for the game.

Exercise 3-9. *Challenge:* *Three Moves*

Create a game with three or more stages. (See Figure 3.4 for an example.) Establish preferences and solve.

Exercise 3-10. *Challenge:* *Three Players*

Create a game with three (or more) actors. Establish preferences and solve.

PUTTING THE PIECES TOGETHER

Exercise 3-11. *Immediate Deterrence*

Much of the writing about crisis and international conflict concerns the conditions under which deterrence succeeds or fails. The following is a typical representation of a decision about immediate deterrence. (Adapted from James Morrow, *Game Theory for Political Scientists* [Princeton: Princeton University Press, 1994].)

The situation is that one actor (the challenger) has made a challenge to a defender. This challenge might involve a demand for territory, economic concessions, or something else that the defender does not want to give up. The defender, in turn, makes a counterthreat to the challenger, saying, "If you press your claim and attack me, I will hurt you." Typically this claim would be something along the lines of, "If you attempt to seize this disputed piece of territory, I will mobilize and attack you militarily." The challenger then has the option to back down or to press the claim. If the challenger presses the claim, then the defender has to choose whether or not to actually carry out the deterrent threat. Just because the defender makes a deterrent threat, the defender will not necessarily carry it out. Figure 3.10 shows this game.

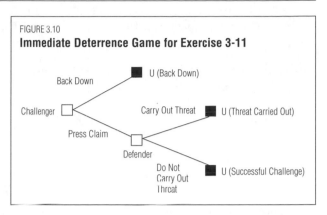

FIGURE 3.10

Immediate Deterrence Game for Exercise 3-11

Here are the relevant options, payoffs, and equations:

$U_{back\ down}$ is what the states get if the challenger backs off. This is certain.

$U_{threat\ carried\ out}$ is what the actors get if the defender actually carries out its deterrent threat.

$U_{successful\ challenge}$ is what the actors get if the defender backs off its deterrent threat and the challenger gets what the challenger wants.

$P_{carry\ out\ threat}$ is the challenger's belief about the probability that the defender will actually carry out the threat.

a) Write the relevant expected utility equations that we would need to solve to determine whether a challenger backs down or presses a claim. (*Hint:* You need two equations.)

b) Under what condition will the challenger press ahead with the challenge? That is, what part of the equations must be larger than another for deterrence to fail?

_____

_____

c) What values in the game could the defender manipulate to make the challenger more likely to back down? How could the defender do this in the real world?

_____

_____

_____

Credibility in Immediate Deterrence

Consider the situation of immediate deterrence we considered in Figure 3.10. How credible does the defender have to be to prevent the challenger from moving ahead? That is, what value must $p_{threat\ carried\ out}$ take before the challenger chooses not to act?

d) Set the relevant choices equal to each other, then solve algebraically for the condition of interest. (*Hint:* You are looking to create an expression of the form "$p_{threat\ carried\ out} = \ldots$")

e) Suppose we are in a situation where the utility values for the challenger are as follows:

$$U_{successful\ challenge} = 450$$

$$U_{threat\ carried\ out} = -800$$

$$U_{back\ down} = 2200$$

What is the critical probability that the defender will carry out its threat that makes the challenger indifferent between backing down and continuing? Use these values to solve for the critical value of $p_{threat\ carried\ out}$.

The Causes of War: Structural Accounts

War versus Negotiation

Exercise 4-1. *Uncertainty as a Cause of War*

Consider again the case of negotiations between Israel and the Palestinians over territory that *Principles* presents at the start of Chapter 4. The two sides can propose some distribution of territory, x, which we can interpret as a percentage of the territory that the Palestinians receive in a settlement. Ideally, then, the Palestinians would like 100 percent of the land, or $x = 1$, and the Israelis' ideal point is at $x = 0$ $(1 - x = 0)$.[1] If the two sides fight, winning has a utility of 1 for the side that wins, since it gets all of the territory; the losing side gets 0. No matter the outcome, both sides pay a cost, k, for fighting.

Expected Values for War

a) Write an expression to show the probability of an Israeli victory.

b) What is the Palestinians' expected utility for war? Write the complete EU expression and then simplify. Explain your answer on the line below (interpret the math in English).

_____

_____

_____

c) What is Israel's expected utility for war? Write the complete EU expression and then simplify. Explain your answer on the line below (interpret the math in English).

_____

_____

_____

Finding Acceptable Settlements

d) Let's consider the case of the Palestinians. According to the logic presented in Chapter 3, actors should choose the option that gives them the highest utility or expected utility. In this case, then, the Palestinians should accept

---

[1] All of these variable names match those in *Principles*.

a settlement proposal of *x* if its utility is at least as much as their expected utility for war. Write an inequality to show this relationship. (Assume that if the values for the two options are equal—that is, the Palestinians are *indifferent* between the two—they will choose to take the sure thing, *x*, over the risky option of war. In other words, the sign should be "greater than or equal to.") Explain your expression on the lines below.

_____

_____

_____

_____

e) Assume for now that both sides will incur a cost of $k = 0.1$ for fighting. Solving your inequality for a range of *p* values, then, will give us a corresponding range of *x* values that show us the Palestinians' minimum acceptable proposals for the current level of costs. Complete Table 4.1 to find those minimum acceptable *x* values.

f) Graph your findings in Figure 4.1. (*Hint:* Notice that the horizontal axis is *p*, the Palestinians' probability of winning, and the vertical axis is our outcome variable, which is *x* in this case.) This line represents the minimum *x* (proposed settlement) that Palestinians should accept, given those costs and probabilities of victory. Shade the region of the figure that represents all acceptable agreements.

TABLE 4.1

Palestinian Values for Settlement and War

p	k	Smallest x
0.1	0.1	
0.2	0.1	
0.3	0.1	
0.4	0.1	
0.5	0.1	
0.6	0.1	
0.7	0.1	
0.8	0.1	
0.9	0.1	

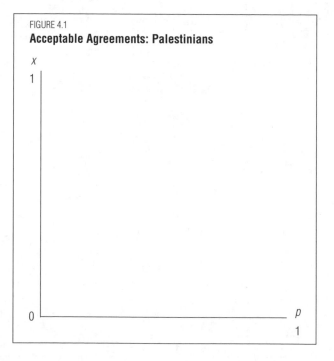

FIGURE 4.1
Acceptable Agreements: Palestinians

g) Now show the inequality for Israel's choices.

h) As you did for the Palestinians, complete Table 4.2 to find the Israelis' acceptable settlements for $k = 0.1$.

TABLE 4.2

Israeli Values for Settlement and War

p	k	x	k'	x'
0.1	0.1			
0.2	0.1			
0.3	0.1			
0.4	0.1			
0.5	0.1			
0.6	0.1			
0.7	0.1			
0.8	0.1			
0.9	0.1			

i) Graph your results in Figure 4.2; label this line as k. Shade the region that represents all potential agreements that the Israelis will accept. (*Hint:* Do the values of x that you found represent the *smallest* values of x that Israel will accept, or do they represent the *largest* values of x? Think about what value of x represents the Israelis' ideal point.)

j) What happens if k changes? Select a new cost of fighting, k'; complete the k' and Smallest x' columns and graph your answers in a different color on Figure 4.2. Label this line k'.

k) Explain what happens to the line of acceptable agreements as k changes. Which way does the line move? As costs increase, do more—or fewer—potential agreements become acceptable? Why? (*Hint:* Think in terms of the variables in your inequality and the total amount of land available, which is 1.)

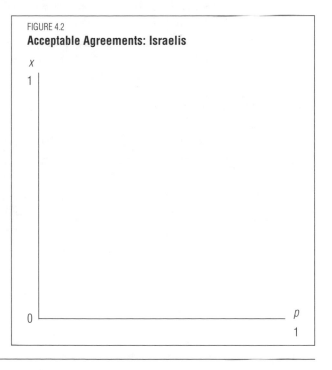

FIGURE 4.2

Acceptable Agreements: Israelis

More Realistic Assumptions about Uncertainty

l) Our earlier assumption that the two sides share a common set of perceptions about the likelihood of winning is probably not one that holds up in the real world. Let's adopt a more realistic assumption that the two sides have different perceptions of the probability of a Palestinian victory (i.e., the value of p). Select one value of p for the Palestinians from Table 4.1 above, and one value of p for the Israelis from Table 4.2. Note these values below Figure 4.3 next to p_P and p_I, along with the value of k (here, 0.1) and the corresponding x values for both sides.

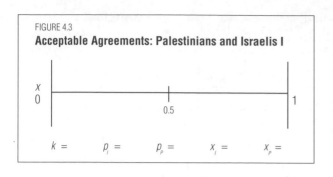

FIGURE 4.3
Acceptable Agreements: Palestinians and Israelis I

x
0 ———————————————— 1
0.5

$k =$ $p_I =$ $p_P =$ $x_I =$ $x_P =$

Next, use Figure 4.3 to show the range of acceptable deals. Start by locating x_P on the horizontal axis. Would the Palestinians accept deals to the left of that point or to the right of that point? Draw an arrow over (or highlight) the set of deals acceptable to the Palestinians. Repeat this process for the Israelis: locate x_I, determine whether the Israelis would accept points to the left or the right, and draw an arrow or highlight. (If you're highlighting, please use different colors and provide a key.) (*Hint:* Use Figure 4.1 in *Principles* as a guide if you're confused.)

Do any possible deals exist in this picture? If so, where are they? How can you identify possible deals just from looking at the figure? If possible deals exist for you, indicate this set of possible deals—known as the *zone of agreement*—on Figure 4.3. How large is the zone of agreement in this case, if you have one?

_____

_____

_____

m) Let's repeat this process, but this time we're going to look for a case in which *no* possible agreements exist. Select a value of p for one party, insert this in the row below Figure 4.4, and circle it to show that you're starting with this value. Complete the k and x values as well, then graph your starting party's set of acceptable deals. (Continue to assume that the parties share a common estimate of $k = 0.1$.)

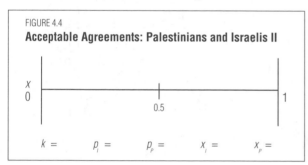

FIGURE 4.4
Acceptable Agreements: Palestinians and Israelis II

x
0 ———————————————— 1
0.5

$k =$ $p_I =$ $p_P =$ $x_I =$ $x_P =$

Now consider the table you made above for the other party and consider what the figure would look like if no zone of agreement existed. Select, note, and graph a value of p for the other party that results in no possible deals. How do you know that no zone of agreement exists here? Given the value of p for the first party that you selected, what is the minimum value of p for the second party that will eliminate the zone of agreement?

_____

_____

_____

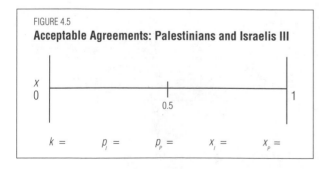

FIGURE 4.5
Acceptable Agreements: Palestinians and Israelis III

x
0 ———————————————— 1
0.5

$k =$ $p_I =$ $p_P =$ $x_I =$ $x_P =$

n) Consider a case in which the parties do share a common estimate of the probability of a Palestinian victory (that is, $p_P = p_I$. Find a value of k that results in no deals acceptable to either party. Indicate the appropriate values and graph your answer in Figure 4.5. (*Hint:* You may want to make a table on scrap paper to experiment; if you do this, please turn it in with your assignment.)

Exercise 4-2. *Commitment Problems as a Cause of War*

Commitment problems occur when one side is reluctant to accept a deal because it fears the other side may have incentives to defect from the deal in the future. Several variants of commitment problems exist. The first, as

Principles describes, is related to having a first strike advantage. If a side can benefit from striking first at its opponent, then settlement proposals aren't credible. Both sides know the other will have an incentive to break the deal by striking first to capture more gains than it achieved in the settlement. A second variant involves agreements in which the settlement itself induces changes in the relative power of the parties. If the settlement in time t increases Country A's power in time $t + 1$, then A has no reason to continue to uphold the deal after time $t + 1$. Now that it is stronger, it has the ability to demand more concessions from Country B, and these concessions will make it stronger in time $t + 2$. Under these conditions, B should never accept a proposed settlement because A will defect from the agreement in the future. Finally, the third variant addresses the problem of disarmament. If A and B sign an agreement that includes disarmament provisions, both sides have incentives to cheat on that agreement. Disarming when you are unsure that your opponent is disarming as well would make you very vulnerable to defection by the other side. Upholding the deal here by disarming could be very costly: a surprise attack could leave you unable to defend yourself. This problem is most commonly found in civil wars, but it also may occur in interstate wars.

Let's continue with the previous example. Assume that a deal to split the disputed territory has already been proposed. The Palestinians now face a choice whether to accept the proposed settlement or to fight. If they choose to fight, Nature then decides the outcome: the Palestinians win with probability p, and they lose with probability $(1 - p)$.

If the Palestinians choose to accept the deal, Israel can either choose to uphold the deal, or it can renege (go back on the deal and use force to seize the ceded land). If the deal sticks, the Palestinians get x, and the Israelis get the remaining land. If Israel reneges on the agreement, then both sides use force and incur the cost k. Since the Palestinians have disarmed in response to the agreement, though, they are unable to defend themselves. They lose all of the ceded territory for sure in this case. What should the Palestinians do?

a)   Draw an extensive form game to depict the situation described above. The game's payoffs should involve the variables x, p, and k.

b)   As we've done before, we solve by backwards induction. Starting from the right, we'll skip the Nature node for now and look at the Israelis' move. When will the Israelis choose to uphold the deal? According to the logic we learned in Chapters 2 and 3, they will do so when their payoffs from upholding it exceed their payoffs from reneging. Write an inequality to represent the situation in which Israel will uphold the agreement, and reduce your expression to simplest terms. Then, on the lines below, explain the expression you found.

c) Now think about a case in which the inequality is satisfied—that is, one in which Israel prefers to uphold the agreement. What is the Palestinians' utility (payoff) for accepting the deal in this case, when Israel prefers to uphold the agreement? Explain your answer.

_____

_____

_____

d) What about a case in which the inequality is not satisfied—one in which Israel prefers to renege on the agreement. What is the Palestinians' utility in this case? Explain your answer.

_____

_____

e) Now find the Palestinians' expected utility for fighting. Simplify as far as possible.

f) According to the concepts we learned in Chapter 4, the Palestinians will fight when doing so has a higher expected utility than settling does. Write the inequality that shows the Palestinians' expected utility from fighting versus the utility of settling *if* they believe that the inequality in part b of this exercise is satisfied and the Israelis will uphold the agreement. Simplify your answer and explain it below.

_____

_____

_____

g) What if the Palestinians believe that the inequality in part b is not satisfied and expect that Israel will renege? Write the inequality that the Palestinians would solve to determine whether to fight or accept under these circumstances. Simplify your answer and explain it below.

_____

_____

_____

h) Consider your responses to parts f and g. Why might the Palestinians choose to fight here, even when a deal is offered?

_____

_____

_____

i) *Challenge* Would the Palestinians ever choose to fight even if they expect Israel to uphold the deal? If so, for what range of x, p, k, or combination of these would they prefer to fight?

_____

_____

_____

STRUCTURAL EXPLANATIONS OF WAR

Exercise 4-3. *Stability in Multipolar Systems*

Create two international systems with the characteristics described below. List the states and their power allocations in the work space below the question. Then, on the lines below each system, determine if it is stable (in the neorealist sense of the word). If it is unstable, which states are inessential? If it is stable, identify the different blocking coalitions that could form.

a) Think of a five-state international system that has 100 units of power. Assign those units as:
   State A: day of your birth (e.g., Valentine's Day = 14)
   State B: sum of the digits of your house number
   State C: sum of the digits of your current phone number (keep adding the digits until the number is less than 40)
   State D and State E: Divide all remaining units of power across these two states in any manner you wish.

_____

_____

_____

b) Now think of a second five-state international system has 200 units of power. Assign those units as:
   State A: sum of the digits of your GPA
   State B: last two digits of your student ID number

State C: the number of college credits you've completed (not counting the current term)
State D and State E: Divide all remaining units of power across these two states in any manner that you wish.

_____

_____

_____

Exercise 4-4.   *Essential and Inessential States*

Over time, quite a few once-essential states have disappeared, and other states have become essential. Make a list below of inessential states that have become essential or once-essential states that have become inessential and have possibly disappeared. (Check Appendix A of *Principles* to brush up on history if you need some ideas.) Then, look at your list for patterns in why states became essential or inessential. Make a hypothesis for why states become inessential, and make a second hypothesis for why they become essential. Briefly discuss the logic behind your hypotheses and identify two or three cases from your lists that fit your hypotheses.

Became Essential: Became Inessential:

Hypothesis for becoming inessential:

Hypothesis for becoming essential:

_____

_____

_____

_____

_____

Exercise 4-5.   *British and U.S. Hegemonic Norms*

a) Great Britain is often considered to be the hegemonic power of the nineteenth century. What rules or norms of international conduct did Britain try to enforce around the world? (*Hint:* Consult Appendix A of *Principles* if you need a history refresher.)

_____

_____

_____

b) The United States is the post–cold war hegemonic power or, in power transition terms, the state at the top of the power pyramid. What are some of the rules or norms of international conduct that the United States tries to enforce around the world today?

_____

_____

_____

c) World War II is frequently interpreted as a failed attempt by Germany to replace Britain as the hegemon. Think about a counterfactual world in which Germany won World War II and rules northern Europe and Russia while Italy rules southern Europe and North Africa. The United States has retreated back into isolationism. Give several examples of *international* norms that might have emerged in a fascist-dominated postwar world. (*Hint:* Think about the key norms of the postwar liberal capitalist hegemony of the United States. What would be different?)

_____

_____

_____

_____

_____

Example 4-6. *Proportional Reduction in Error*

A statistic known as the proportional reduction in error helps us compare the empirical accuracy of different theories. Let's use a simple numerical example to explore this useful tool.

Brussels, Belgium, is a very rainy place. In fact, Brussels gets rain (or snow) about three hundred days a year, leaving only sixty-five days of sun—or at least no precipitation. If you were asked to predict the weather in Brussels on any given day, your best guess would be to pick the modal (most frequently occurring) category: rain. About 5/6 of the time (82 percent, to be exact), you would be right. The other 18 percent of the time you would have predicted erroneously. We call this prediction of the most common outcome the *null hypothesis.*

Another "theory" predicts a six-day weather pattern: rain, rain, rain, rain, rain, sun. Data show that this theory correctly predicts 322 days, or about 91 percent of the time. About 9 percent of the predictions are incorrect.

To calculate the *proportionate reduction in error* (PRE) of our weather pattern theory, we compare the share of cases (days, in this example) we predicted incorrectly using the theory with how many cases we predicted incorrectly just using the null hypothesis. The null hypothesis, "the modal outcome occurs in every case," predicts correctly 82 percent of the time. Our weather pattern theory predicts correctly 91 percent of the time. The modal category, as we saw above, contains 82 percent of the outcomes.

The general formula for PRE is:

$$(\% \text{ correct by theory} - \% \text{ correct by null}) / (100 - \% \text{ of cases correct by null})$$

Inserting our values, we find

$$(91\% - 82\%) / (100\% - 82\%) = 9 / 18 = 1/2 \text{ or } 50\%$$

The weather pattern theory improves on the null hypothesis by making half as many predictive errors as the null. We have reduced our errors by 50 percent—hence the term PRE.

TABLE 4.3
Empirical Evidence for the Power Transition Theory

Does War Occur?	Power Is Unequal	Power Is Equal and Challenger Is Not Overtaking Hegemon	Power Is Equal and Challenger Is Overtaking Hegemon
No	4	6	5
Yes	0	0	5

Source: Adapted from A.F.K. Organski and Jacek Kugler, *The War Ledger* (Chicago: University of Chicago Press, 1980), 52, Table 1.7.

Exercise 4-7. *Measuring PRE in Power Transition Theory*

a)   What is the PRE (Proportionate Reduction in Error) gained from the power transition theory, as indicated by the evidence in Table 4.3? (*Hint:* Determine carefully what represents the outcome, rows or columns, and which outcome occurs most frequently.)

b)   Compare your findings to the results in Table 4.3 in *Principles*. What should we infer when different statistical tests legitimately lead to different conclusions about a theory's explanatory and predictive potential?

_____

_____

_____

_____

CHAPTER 5

STRATEGIC THEORIES OF WAR

THE INTERNATIONAL INTERACTION GAME: WALK-THROUGH

Figure 5.1 in *Principles of International Politics* presents the International Interaction Game (IIG). The IIG begins with a move by state A in a pair of countries A and B. As in our previous games of deterrence, A has the opportunity to either make a demand of B or not make a demand. If A does not make a demand, B will have an option to make a demand, and another subgame follows. But if A does make a demand, then B can either give in—leading to an acquiescence by B—or can make a counter demand. Such a counter demand might just mean saying "no," or it might mean making a counterproposal of some sort. If B makes a counter demand, then the IIG enters what is labeled the "crisis subgame." The crisis subgame is labeled as such because at that point both players have made demands, fitting with the characterizations of an international crisis that must be resolved by negotiation, use of force, or surrender.

Within the crisis subgame, the key decision by each player is whether or not to attack. A, who made the first demand in the game, has the first opportunity to attack. If A does attack B, then B has two options. B may retaliate, leading to a war in which A will have some advantage because A attacked first. Or B may decide to surrender, capitulating to A. One of the key assumptions of the game is that from B's perspective, capitulation by B is always worse than acquiescence by B. If B is going to surrender, then B prefers to do it early in the interaction before the interaction becomes public and B's retreat is obvious.

If A does not attack in the first move of the crisis subgame and instead offers to negotiate with B, then B has a different choice. B may accept the negotiation offered by A, leading to a peaceful resolution, but one in which the game assumes the outcome of negotiations is determined by power relationships. Or B may instead decide to attack A, perhaps using the excuse of A's demand as justification. A then must decide how to respond, either retaliating and fighting a war in which B has an advantage from going first or surrendering to B, giving up the object in dispute but avoiding the costs of a war.

Going back to the very first node of the game, if A does not demand something of B, B has its own chance to issue a demand. If B does not make a demand, then neither player has made a demand and the status quo results. But if B does make a demand, then the game enters a lower subgame that is the flipside of the upper subgame. The only difference between the top and bottom subgames from this point forward is that the actors are reversed. For instance, if A does not issue a counter demand, then A acquiesces (before it was B), and so on.

SOLVING THE INTERNATIONAL INTERACTION GAME USING BACKWARDS INDUCTION

If we know the preferences of the states playing the IIG, we can solve the game and predict the outcome just by using backwards induction. For easier presentation, I use the following notation and terms in these exercises:

OUTCOMES
SQ: Status Quo
Nego: Negotiation
Acq_A: Acquiescence by A
Acq_B: Acquiescence by B

Cap_A: Capitulation by A
Cap_B: Capitulation by B
War_A: War Started by A
War_B: War Started by B

We distinguish here between two types of "giving in" to indicate the sequence of moves that preceded this action. "Acquiescence" means giving in to a demand prior to any actor making threats to use force. "Capitulation" means giving in after being attacked by the other actor.

Types of Players

In *Principles* the terms *dove* and *hawk* refer to whether states prefer to negotiate with their rivals or force opponents to capitulate, respectively. The text also examines states that prefer war to capitulation or capitulation to war. I label these two types of states retaliator and surrenderer. A retaliator prefers to respond to an attack with a war rather than capitulate. A surrenderer prefers to give in (capitulate) rather than fight. Finally, a pacific dove is one who is both a dove and a surrenderer.

In summary, state A is a:

- *dove* if it prefers to negotiate with a rival rather than force its opponent to capitulate (Nego > Cap_B);
- *hawk* if it prefers to force a rival to capitulate rather than negotiate (Cap_B > Nego);
- *retaliator* if it prefers to respond to an attack with a war rather than capitulate (War_B > Cap_A);
- *surrenderer* if it prefers to capitulate in the face of an attack rather than fight a war (Cap_A > War_B);
- *pacific dove* if it is both a dove and a surrenderer.

Similarly, state B is a:

- *dove* if it prefers to negotiate with a rival rather than force its opponent to capitulate (Nego > Cap_A);
- *hawk* if it prefers to force a rival to capitulate rather than negotiate (Cap_A > Nego);
- *retaliator* if it prefers to respond to an attack with a war rather than capitulate (War_A > Cap_B);
- *surrenderer* if it prefers to capitulate in the face of an attack rather than fight a war (Cap_B > War_A);
- *pacific dove* if it is both a dove and a surrenderer.

Even within these categories, many possible preference orderings could be true for a state that is a hawk, dove, pacific dove, etc. For example, for some state A the ordering Acq_B > Cap_B > Nego > SQ > War_A > Acq_A > Cap_A > War_B is a valid preference ordering for a hawk, but so is Acq_B > SQ > Cap_B > Nego > Acq_A > War_A > Cap_A > War_B. These orderings are different, but both of them satisfy the preference ordering restrictions listed in Table 5.1 of *Principles,* as well as the additional condition for being a hawk. Solving the IIG between two states requires knowing the *exact* ordering for both actors.

Exercise 5-1. *Solving the IIG for Two Particular Hawks*

Suppose we are in a situation in which A's preferences are Acq_B > Cap_B > Nego > SQ > War_A > Acq_A > Cap_A > War_B and B's preferences are Acq_A > Cap_A > Nego > SQ > War_B > War_A > Acq_B > Cap_B.

A and B are both hawks. That is, they both prefer to force a capitulation from a rival rather than negotiate. They also both satisfy the other preference ordering restrictions listed in Table 5.1 of the main text. If you wish, you can verify that all of the conditions in Table 5.1 are true for these two states. You can also read through the outcomes and verify that these are reasonable orderings for the states to have. In this case, each state most prefers to see the other back down early; the second-best outcome is to have the opponent back down under the threat of war. Negotiation is next preferred and is better than the status quo. Both A and B want some kind of change in the status quo, as any favorable change is beneficial, but the status quo is preferred to war. Finally, a war started by A is better than giving in to B's demands, and the same is true for B with regard to A.

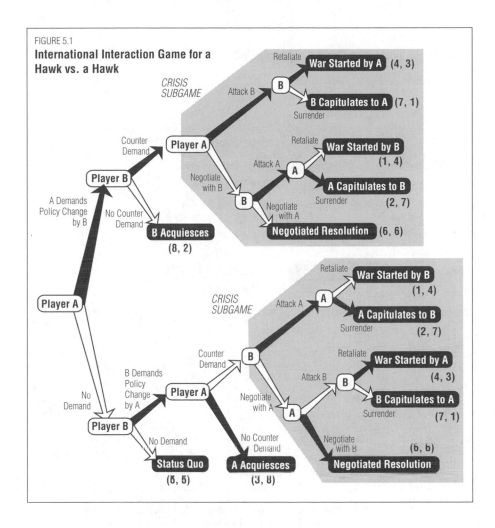

FIGURE 5.1

International Interaction Game for a Hawk vs. a Hawk

Figure 5.1 presents this game along with the backwards induction solution. Note that in contrast to Figure 5.1 in the main text, this game has ordinal payoffs written next to each terminal node, numbered from 1 (worst) through 8 (best). Following the usual convention, A's payoffs are listed before B's. For instance, the outcome Acq_B, an acquiescence by B, is the most-preferred option for state A, and the next-to-worst outcome for state B, and so the payoff pair in the game for the "B acquiesces" outcome is (8, 2).

a) Verify that the payoffs written in Figure 5.1 reflect the preference orderings listed above.

b) Trace through the backwards induction of the game and verify that the equilibrium outcome is a war started by A.

Exercise 5-2. *Solving the IIG for a Hawk vs. a Dove*

Suppose that A is a hawk, but B is now a dove. Suppose A's preferences are $Acq_B > SQ > Cap_B > Nego > Acq_A > War_A > Cap_A > War_B$ and B's are $Acq_A > Nego > Cap_A > SQ > Acq_B > Cap_B > War_B > War_A$. In this situation, B considers war to be the worst of all possible options. What will happen?

a) Write in the payoffs that reflect these preference orderings for the two players in Figure 5.2. Solve the game in Figure 5.2 by backwards induction. What is the equilibrium outcome?

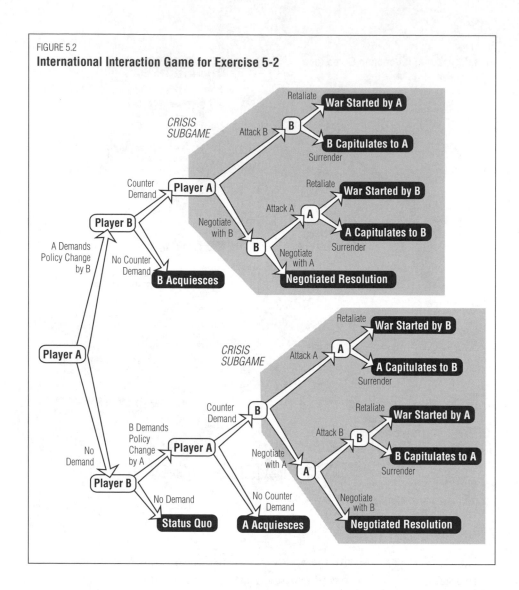

FIGURE 5.2
International Interaction Game for Exercise 5-2

Exercise 5-3. *Solving the IIG for Two Doves*

What if both players are doves and prefer to negotiate rather than demand capitulation? Can we then achieve a peaceful outcome? Suppose that A and B are both doves. A's preference ordering is $Acq_B > SQ > Nego > Cap_B > Acq_A > War_A > Cap_A > War_B$, whereas B's preferences are $Acq_A > SQ > Nego > Cap_A > Acq_B > War_B > Cap_B > War_A$. What will happen?

a) Write in the payoffs that reflect these preference orderings for the two players in Figure 5.3.

b) Solve the game in Figure 5.3 by backwards induction. What is the equilibrium outcome?

Exercise 5-4. *Solving the IIG for Two Different Hawks*

Many different preference orderings could exist in which the two states are still hawks or doves or pacific doves or any other general characterization we develop. Sometimes changing the other elements of the preference ordering will affect the expected outcome of the IIG; other times it will not. The following game is between two slightly different hawks than were in Exercise 5-1. Suppose A's preferences are $Acq_B > Cap_B > Nego > War_A > Acq_A > SQ > Cap_A > War_B$, whereas B's are $Acq_A > SQ > Cap_A > Nego > War_B > War_A > Acq_B > Cap_B$. What will happen?

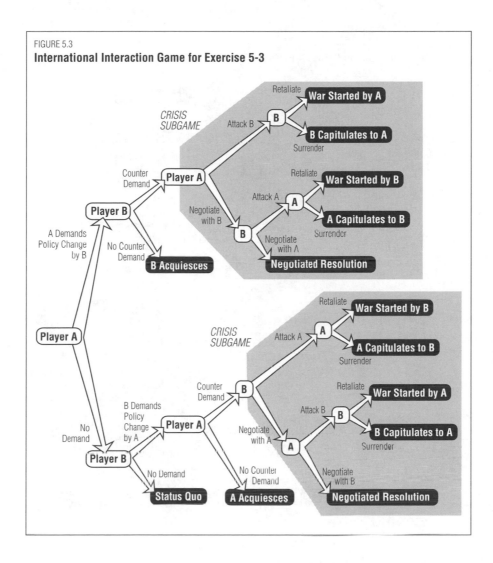

FIGURE 5.3
International Interaction Game for Exercise 5-3

a)   Write in the payoffs that reflect these preference orderings for the two players in Figure 5.4.

b)   Solve the game in Figure 5.4 by backwards induction. What is the equilibrium outcome?

Exercise 5-5.   *Solving the IIG for Two Different Doves*

In Exercise 5-3 we saw the interaction of two doves that resulted in a continuation of the status quo (if you solved the problem correctly). This suggests that an interaction between two doves is likely to end peacefully. But we cannot conclude this from assessing just one preference ordering within the dove type. As stated in Exercise 5-4, we can obtain different outcomes within the same categories of states given slightly different preference orderings. Consider the following two states that are still doves. A's preferences are $Acq_B > Nego > Cap_B > SQ > War_A > Acq_A > Cap_A > War_B$, whereas B's preferences are $Acq_A > Nego > Cap_A > SQ > War_B > Acq_B > Cap_B > War_A$.

a)   Write in the payoffs that reflect these preference orderings for the two players in Figure 5.5.

b)   Solve the game in Figure 5.5 by backwards induction. What is the equilibrium outcome?

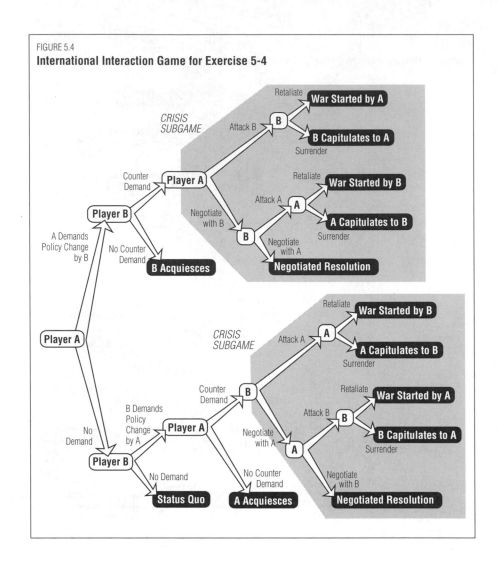

FIGURE 5.4
International Interaction Game for Exercise 5-4

Exercise 5-6.   *Uncertainty and War in the International Interaction Game*

As some of the previous examples show, war can occur as an outcome of the IIG through several different paths. There are many different preference orderings that can lead states into war. *Principles* makes the point that according to the strategic perspective, war can happen even without uncertainty, and the examples show this. In all cases, the players knew each other's preferences and still found themselves at war. Exercise 5-6 shows a very dramatic example of this phenomenon.

Consider a case in which the two players know what each other wants (they know each other's preferences) and know that they both really, really like the status quo. Consider an interaction in which A's preferences are Acq_B > SQ > Nego > Cap_B > War_A > Acq_A > Cap_A > War_B, whereas B's preferences are Acq_A > SQ > Cap_A > Nego > War_B > War_A > Acq_B > Cap_B. What is the solution?

a)   Write in the payoffs that reflect these preference orderings for the two players in Figure 5.6.

b)   Solve the game in Figure 5.6 by backwards induction.

c)   What is the outcome of the game? Why does it seem so surprising?

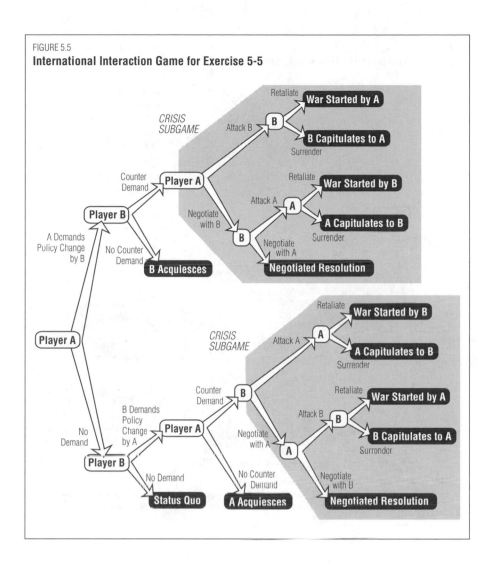

FIGURE 5.5
International Interaction Game for Exercise 5-5

Pacific Doves and War

Principles discusses circumstances under which a dove, even a weak pacific dove, might attack other states. When a pacific dove is uncertain what type of player it is facing, sometimes making a challenge is in the dove's interest. It hopes that its opponent will back down early, and it hopes to avoid a challenge by the opponent that would lead to the dove backing down itself. Of course, that pacific dove may end up with an unintended outcome if it challenges a state that resists. Here are some of the circumstances that a pacific dove might face in dealing with other states. As we will see, the outcome of interactions involving pacific doves is critically dependent on the kind of opponent it faces.

Sometimes, even when it is facing a nasty opponent, it can be in the interest of a pacific dove to make a demand and initiate a crisis, because it might get lucky.

Exercise 5-7. *Solving the IIG for a Pacific Dove vs. a Hawk Retaliator I*

Circumstance 1: Pacific doves can force opponents to back down. Sometimes a pacific dove can end up in a favorable circumstance when it initiates a crisis by making a demand. Consider the following situation between a

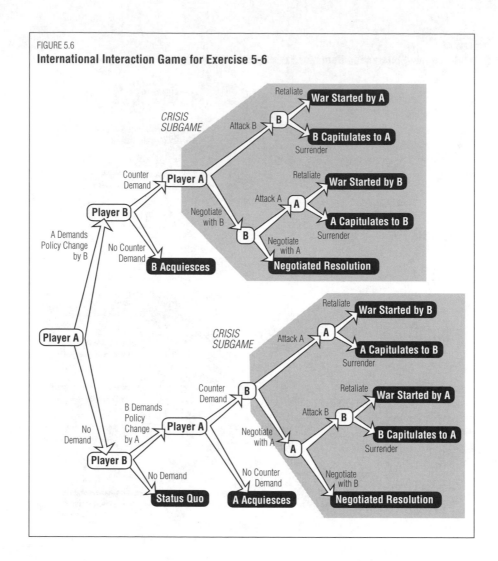

FIGURE 5.6
International Interaction Game for Exercise 5-6

pacific dove and the following particular hawk, which prefers to fight rather than capitulate (a hawk retaliator). This is what a pacific dove is hoping for if it makes a demand.

$$\text{A's preferences are } Acq_B > SQ > Nego > Acq_A > Cap_B > War_A > Cap_A > War_B.$$

$$\text{B's preferences are } Acq_A > SQ > Cap_A > Nego > War_B > Acq_B > War_A > Cap_B.$$

a) Write in the payoffs that reflect these preference orderings for the two players in Figure 5.7.

b) Solve the game in Figure 5.7 by backwards induction. What is the equilibrium outcome?

Exercise 5-8. *Solving the IIG for a Pacific Dove vs. a Hawk Retaliator II*

Circumstance 2: Other times when a pacific dove issues a demand, however, it may be forced to back down.

$$\text{A's preferences are } Acq_B > SQ > Nego > Acq_A > Cap_B > War_A > Cap_A > War_B.$$

$$\text{B's preferences are } Acq_A > SQ > Cap_A > Nego > War_B > War_A > Acq_B > Cap_B.$$

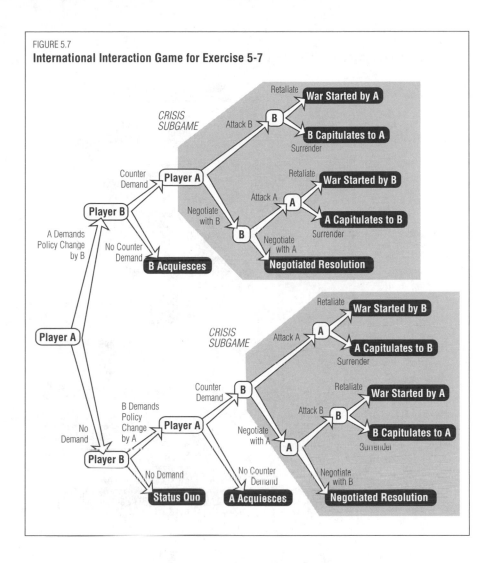

FIGURE 5.7
International Interaction Game for Exercise 5-7

a) Write in the payoffs that reflect these preference orderings for the two players in Figure 5.8.

b) Solve the game in Figure 5.8 by backwards induction. What is the equilibrium outcome?

c) There is one critical difference in the preference orderings in Exercise 5-8 from those in 5-7 that leads to this important change in outcome. What is it? Why does this one small change have such a large effect?

Exercise 5-9. *Solving the IIG for a Pacific Dove vs. a Hawk Retaliator III*

Circumstance 3: Sometimes, pacific doves may even find themselves in wars that they actually started. Note that in this case, both states actually like the status quo as their second-best outcome.

A's preferences are $Acq_B > SQ > Nego > Cap_B > War_A > Acq_A > Cap_A > War_B$.

B's preferences are $Acq_A > SQ > Cap_A > Nego > War_B > War_A > Acq_B > Cap_B$.

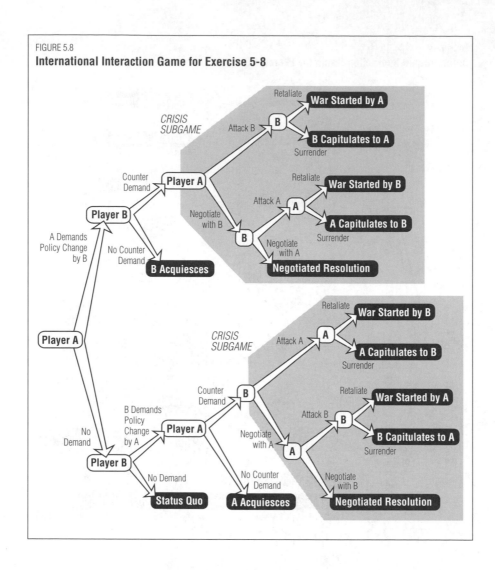

FIGURE 5.8
International Interaction Game for Exercise 5-8

a) Write in the payoffs that reflect these preference orderings for the two players in Figure 5.9.

b) Solve the game in Figure 5.9 by backwards induction. What is the equilibrium outcome?

_____

_____

c) Again, there is one critical difference in the preference orderings in Exercise 5-9 from those in 5-8 that leads to this important change in outcome. What is it? Why does this one small change have such a large effect?

_____

_____

_____

_____

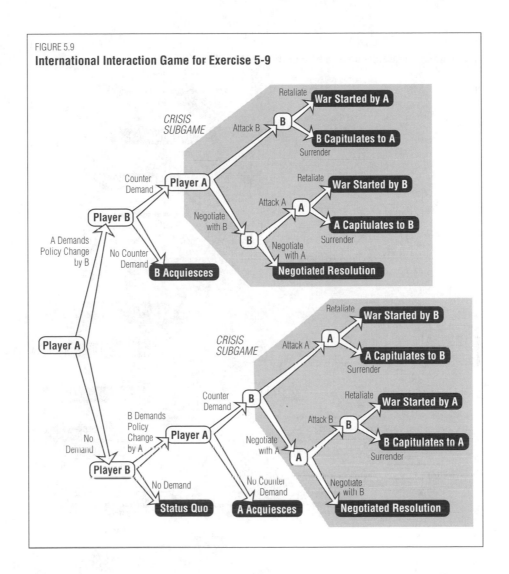

FIGURE 5.9
International Interaction Game for Exercise 5-9

Exercise 5-10. *Solving the IIG for a Pacific Dove vs. a Pacific Dove I*
In this case A and B are pacific doves that both like the status quo.

A's preferences are $Acq_B > SQ > Nego > Cap_B > Acq_A > Cap_A > War_A > War_B$.

B's preferences are $Acq_A > SQ > Nego > Acq_B > Cap_A > Cap_B > War_B > War_A$.

a) Write in the payoffs that reflect these preference orderings for the two players in Figure 5.10.

b) Solve the game in Figure 5.10 by backwards induction. What is the equilibrium outcome?

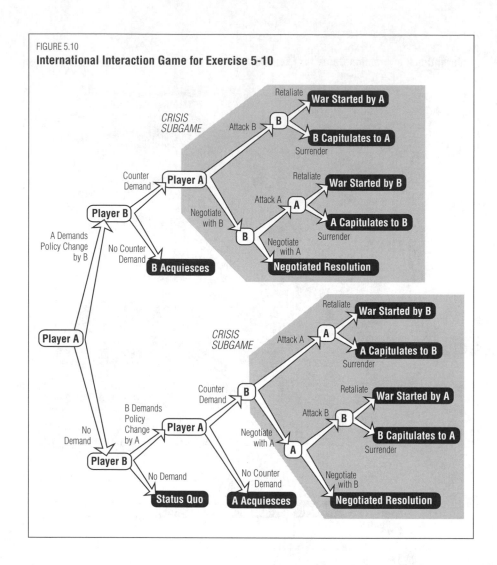

FIGURE 5.10
International Interaction Game for Exercise 5-10

Exercise 5-11. *Solving the IIG for a Pacific Dove vs. a Pacific Dove II*

In this case A and B both prefer to negotiate rather than accept the status quo, and B actually prefers to force A to capitulate rather than accept the status quo.

A's preferences are $Acq_B > Nego > SQ > Cap_B > Acq_A > Cap_A > War_A > War_B$.

B's preferences are $Acq_A > Nego > Cap_A > SQ > Acq_B > Cap_B > War_B > War_A$.

a)   Write in the payoffs that reflect these preference orderings for the two players in Figure 5.11.

b)   Solve the game in Figure 5.11 by backwards induction. What is the equilibrium outcome?

_____

_____

c)   What changes in the preference orderings between Exercises 5-11 and 5-10 lead to this important change in outcome?

_____

_____

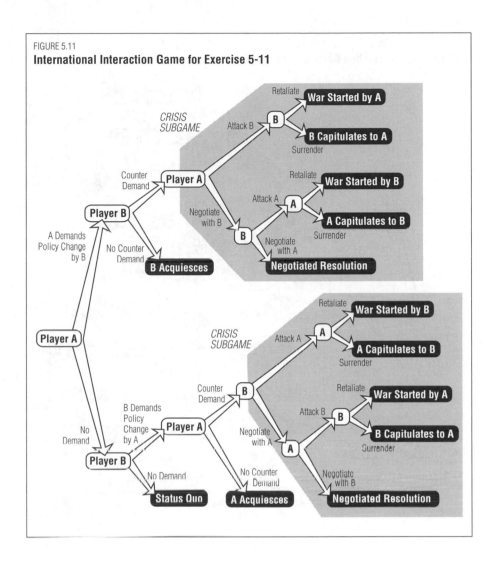

FIGURE 5.11
International Interaction Game for Exercise 5-11

d) Examine your work in Exercises 5-10 and 5-11. When two doves are in a crisis, how do the outcomes differ from interactions involving a hawk and a dove? Two hawks?

_____

_____

_____

EXTENSIONS

Exercise 5-12. *Threats and the Use of Unconventional Weapons*

Apply the resurrection hypothesis to a threat made by a leader in state A to go to war to depose the leader in state B to prevent the leader of state B from using nuclear, chemical, or biological weapons in war. Does the threat of being deposed make the threatened leader more likely, less likely, or equally likely to use unconventional weapons in war? Explain your answer in terms of the resurrection hypothesis or the logic of the IIG.

_____

_____

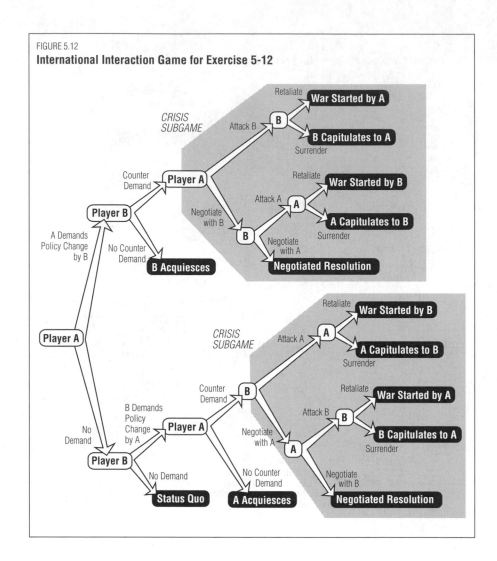

FIGURE 5.12
International Interaction Game for Exercise 5-12

Exercise 5-13.   *Challenge: Is Capitulation Logical?*

Can a capitulation by player A or player B be an equilibrium outcome of the IIG under complete and perfect information? Support your answer by explaining how the logic of the game, given its assumptions, determined your response. If possible, provide a pair of preference orderings—ones that are allowable under the domestic IIG—that would produce this effect. Use Figure 5.12 for your work, if necessary.

Chapter 6

The Democratic Peace

Domestic Political Institutions and War

Exercise 6-1. *Resource Allocation and War Effort*

Say that you are the leader of a country, and you have decided to go to war with a neighbor. You must now decide how much of your national revenue, R, you want to put toward the war effort. For simplicity, let's restrict the choices right now to all (100%) or nothing (0%). At the end of the war, members of your winning coalition will decide whether to reselect you for another period in office.

If you choose to put $R = 0$ toward the war effort, you will surely lose (which has utility 0), but you will still have all of your revenue to distribute to members of your winning coalition, w, as private goods.[1]

If you choose to put all of your revenue, $R = 1$, into fighting the war, you will surely win. Winning the war has a value V that is equal to some amount of public goods, v, plus some amount of spoils of war, r. Public goods are indivisible over the entire population, but the spoils are divided among the members of w.

No matter your revenue allocation decision ($R = 1$ or $R = 0$), war is costly. Each member of w will lose a *per capita* cost of war, k, as the cost of fighting. Because you are a strategic politician, you look ahead down the sequence of interactions; you know that you face reselection at the end of the war. By backwards induction, then, the best choice for you at this resource allocation decision node is the one that makes members of w prefer to reselect you. Thus, we will focus on their payoff for war rather than yours, the leader's.

a)   Write an expression that represents a member of w's utility for war if the leader chooses $R = 0$.

$U_w [R=0] =$

b)   Write an expression that represents a member of w's utility for war if the leader chooses $R = 1$.

$U_w [R=1] =$

c)   As a leader who wants to retain office in the next period, you prefer to put resources into fighting the war if, for members of the winning coalition, the utility of $R = 1$ exceeds the utility of $R = 0$. Write the equation that expresses this relationship.

d)   Consider the equation you wrote in part c of this exercise. How big does the public goods component of victory have to be for you to allocate all your resources to war? (*Hint:* Express your answer in terms of other variables and simplify as far as possible.)

---

[1]I use the small w here for convenience; this does not imply that your winning coalition is small.

e) Assume that all of the variables in your equation are fixed (held constant) except for w. What happens to the value of the expression involving R, r, and w as w becomes very large? What happens to the value of that expression as w gets very small?

_____

_____

_____

f) For a country with a very small w, which side of the inequality you wrote in part d is likely to be larger? Given this, and given the preference of leaders with small ws to use private goods to reward members of w, are we likely to see a lot of autocracies putting their resources toward fighting in a war? Why or why not?

_____

_____

_____

_____

g) For a country with a very large W, which side of the inequality you wrote in part d is likely to be larger? Given this, and given the preference of leaders with large Ws to use public goods to reward members of W, are we likely to see a lot of democracies putting their resources toward fighting in a war? Why or why not?

_____

_____

_____

_____

Exercise 6-2.   *Exploring Relationships in the Resource Allocation Model*

This exercise builds on the expressions you wrote in parts a and b of Exercise 6-1 and on the discussion in Chapter 6 of *Principles*. You will need a ruler or straightedge, a calculator, and several colored pencils, pens, or highlighters. For each section, evaluate the appropriate expression from above for the given values and plot the utility on the axes provided.

The Components of Winning: Values of r and v

a) Complete the table below. Evaluate the utility of your $R = 1$ expression from part b above using $k = 2$ and $w = 5$.

b) Graph the values you found in Figure 6.1. For simplicity, the horizontal axis is $v / v + r$ (the share of V that is public goods).[2]

TABLE 6.1

The Components of Winning

v	r	U	v/v+r
0	10		
3	7		
5	5		
7	3		
10	0		

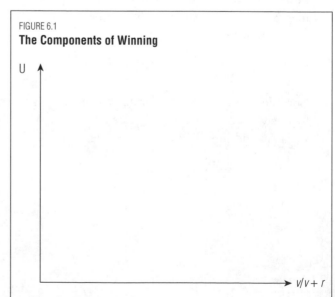

FIGURE 6.1
The Components of Winning

U

v/v+r

---

[2]If we didn't do this, you'd be trying to graph in three dimensions, which is not a lot of fun.

c) Consider the graph that you just drew. The line you plotted is a set of points. Why is that line useful? What do those points mean or tell us? (*Hint:* Think back to the expression you used to generate those points. What were you plotting?)

_____

_____

_____

d) What would happen to the line you drew in Figure 6.1 if $k = 1$? If $k = 5$? Add these two lines to your figure in different colors. (Please provide a key for your instructor.) More generally, how do changes in k affect the utility of winning, and how does this appear on the graph?

_____

_____

The Cost of Fighting: Values of k

e) Let's see what happens now as the costs of fighting change. Consider again your expression from part b of the previous exercise, in which $R = 1$. Evaluate this expression in which $r – 4$, $w – 5$, and $v – 6$, for the values of k listed in Table 6.2, then graph your findings in Figure 6.2.

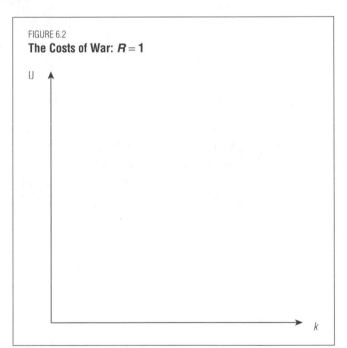

TABLE 6.2

The Costs of Fighting: $R = 1$

k	U	$v' =$___ U	$v'' =$___ U
0			
1			
2			
3			
4			
5			

FIGURE 6.2

The Costs of War: $R = 1$

f) Now try the same thing using the expression from part a of the previous exercise in which the leader puts none of the revenue toward the war effort (i.e., the part of R remaining to be distributed to the members of w is 1). Continue to assume that $w = 5$.

g) Consider your graphs in Figures 6.2 and 6.3. How are they similar? How are they different? How does moving from $R = 1$ to $R = 0$ affect the utility of members of w?

_____

_____

_____

_____

h) Return to your graph in Figure 6.2. How does the value of v affect the utility of war? Select two different values of v and note them next to v' and v'' in Table 6.2. Then, substitute your new values of v and the listed values of k into the expression from part a of Exercise 6-1. Add these two lines to Figure 6.2 in different colors.

TABLE 6.3
The Costs of Fighting: $R = 0$

k	U
0	
1	
2	
3	
4	
5	

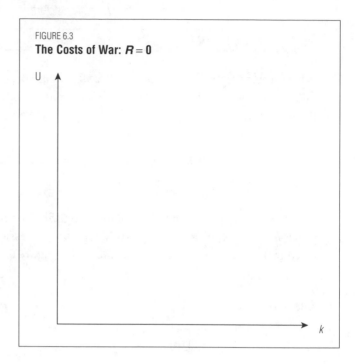

FIGURE 6.3
The Costs of War: $R = 0$

i) Compare Figure 6.3 and the revised version of Figure 6.2. As v increases, does war become more or less valuable for a state that commits resources to war? Consider a state that doesn't commit resources to war ($R = 0$). What is the lowest value of v that can make the utility of war *with* resource commitment greater than the utility of war without resource commitment? Briefly discuss how you found this answer. Does your answer make sense? Why or why not?

_____

_____

_____

_____

Exercise 6-3. *Intermediate Values of Democracy*

We've now manipulated just about all of the variables in *Principles*'s arguments about why states choose to fight. The only variable we haven't examined fully is the core one: democracy. So far, we've treated states as being either fully democratic (big W, big S), or fully autocratic (small w, small s). What happens when states are not fully democratic? For our purposes, we'll interpret that as having a political system with small to moderate sized w but big S.

Revisit the list of seven empirical regularities that comprise the "democratic peace" on pages 180–181 of *Principles*. Identify all of those that will hold and all of the ones that won't (that is, ones in which you expect quasi-democracies to behave differently than full democracies or full autocracies).

a) Which of the items on the list are likely to hold for quasi-democracies? List the numbers of the regularities that you believe will hold for quasi-democracies (ones in which quasi-democracies will behave the same way as full democracies).

b) Which of the items on the list do you think are *not* likely to hold for quasi-democracies? List the numbers of the regularities that you believe will not hold for quasi-democracies (ones in which quasi-democracies will not behave the same way as full democracies).

c) Consider two of the regularities in which you expect different behavior (from part b of this exercise). For each, explain why you think this regularity will not hold for quasi-democracies and what behavior pattern you would expect to see instead. (*Hint:* You might think about this in terms of the variables in our original models. What values would quasi-democracies have, and how might these affect conflict behavior?)

1)

_____

_____

_____

_____

_____

2)

_____

_____

_____

_____

_____

Exercise 6-4. *Quasi-Democracies and Wars*

Two quasi-democracies, Russia and Georgia, fought a war in 2008 over the Georgian territory of South Ossetia. The territory is home to a large number of Russian citizens, thanks to forced migration in the early years of the Soviet Union. It is also a large portion of Georgian territory, however, and it is strategically located in the center of the country in a manner that makes ceding it to Russia (or allowing it significant autonomy) very dangerous to the Georgian state.

The Data

Complete the data table (Table 6.4) below for Russia and Georgia. You may wish to use the CIA World Fact Book (from www.cia.gov), the country profiles provided by the UK's Foreign and Commonwealth Office (www.fco.gov.uk) or the U.S. Department of State (www.state.gov), or similar sites to obtain some of your information. Use the variable definitions below.

- Who is in *W/S*? Identify major social or political groups.
- Size of *W* and *S*? Code this as small, medium, or large.

- Executive attaining office: This variable may have one of two values, selection or election. These terms are drawn from the POLITY project, our most widely used measurement of democracy, and they capture the idea of "Executive Recruitment: Competition."
  - **Election:** Chief executives are typically chosen in or through competitive elections matching two or more major parties or candidates. (Elections may be popular or by an elected assembly.)
  - **Selection:** Chief executives are determined by hereditary succession, designation, or by a combination of both, as in monarchies whose chief minister is chosen by king or court. Examples of pure designative selection are rigged, unopposed elections; repeated replacement of presidents before their terms end; recurrent military selection of civilian executives; selection within an institutionalized single party; recurrent incumbent selection of successors; and repeated election boycotts by the major opposition parties.[3]
- Democracy summary: Consider all the data you reported in parts a–f of this exercise and summarize the level of democracy in each country on a scale of 0–4, with 0 being complete autocracy and 5 being mature democracy.
- Military size: Summarize the size of the military.
- Nature of dispute: Using the definitions and explanations provided in Chapter 4, determine whether each side saw the dispute as one of an indivisible issue, a commitment problem, or a bargaining problem (involving private information and uncertainty). BBC News (www.bbc.co.uk) usually has excellent collections of articles linked together for any crisis or conflict.

TABLE 6.4

Comparing Russia and Georgia

	Russia	Georgia
Political Institutions: a) Who is in *S*?		
b) How big is *S*?		
c) Who is in *W*?		
d) How big is *W*?		
Executives: e) Who is the leader?		
f) How did the leader attain office?		
g) Democracy summary		
Conflict: h) Military size?		
i) Nature of dispute?		

---

[3]These definitions are taken from Monty G. Marshall and Keith Jaggers, *Polity IV Dataset User's Manual.* University of Maryland, College Park: Center for International Development and Conflict Management, 1999, page 19. We thank the authors for permission to reproduce their definitions here.

Comparing the Cases

j) Consider your data table above. To what extent was each leader constrained by his domestic audience? Briefly present some evidence from the case to support your claims.

_____

_____

_____

_____

_____

k) According to our theory about the effects of the size of W and S, which country should have been less constrained in its decision to wage war? Does the evidence from the case support this hypothesis? Briefly present some evidence for or against this hypothesis.

_____

_____

_____

_____

l) Consider your hypotheses from Exercise 6-3 about the democratic peace regularities and quasi-democracies. Which of our "regularities" from this chapter are supported by this case? Which are not supported? How well are your hypotheses from Exercise 6-3 supported by this case? Provide some evidence from the case to support your claims.

_____

_____

_____

_____

_____

m) Consider arguments about the causes of conflict that we discussed in Chapter 4, which you've entered in your table as the "nature of the dispute." Which argument for the cause of the war seems best supported by this particular case? Provide some evidence from the case to support your claims.

_____

_____

_____

_____

_____

CHAPTER 7

CAN TERRORISM BE RATIONAL?

THE RATIONALITY OF TERROR

Exercise 7-1. *Modeling Terrorism*

Principles discusses a game of terrorism that is played between any of three types of social groups and either of two types of governments. What we see from the analysis is that while terrorist activity is sometimes carried out by uncompromising individuals who believe in using violence under any circumstances, and who cannot be reasoned with, in other instances it can result from groups of people who would genuinely be willing to talk if the government would let them. However, perceptions are critical to this process and outcome.

SOCIETAL GROUPS True Believers are committed to violence, even if a government would be willing to talk with them. For them, preferences are Terrorist Act > Good Faith Negotiations > Being Repressed.

Reluctant Terrorists would like to talk, but would rather commit terrorist acts than be repressed by a nasty government. Their preferences are Good Faith Negotiations > Terrorist Act > Being Repressed.

Complacent Opponents would not commit terrorist acts even if they were repressed by a government. They would prefer to talk with a government that might give them what they want, but would accept repression before resorting to violence. Their preferences are Good Faith Negotiations > Being Repressed > Terrorist Act.

GOVERNMENTS One of the problems with a group that wants to conduct negotiations with a government is that, in some countries, groups do not know what kind of government they are facing. The government might be a type that is willing to listen to problems and negotiate an acceptable political solution for the problems raised by the societal group. But the government might also be one that would use the cover of a negotiation to learn the identities of those who question it and repress them.

Responsive Governments prefer Good Faith Negotiations > Repression > Terrorist Target.

Nasty Governments prefer Repression > Good Faith Negotiations > Terrorist Target.

Either type of government prefers to be subject to terrorist attack least, and both prefer repressing a group in society rather than allowing it to conduct terrorist attacks. But they differ in that responsive governments would prefer negotiation to repressing a dissatisfied group in society, whereas a nasty government wants to repress no matter what.

We want to understand what each group in society should do if it wants to be heard. Typically we think that a dissatisfied group should tell its problems to the government in order for the problem to be solved. The alternative is that the group resorts to violence (terrorism) to communicate its message. The difficult part of the decision for a group is that when it goes to the government and offers to talk, it might be met with repression. Depending on the group's type, this may not be an acceptable alternative.

Figures 7.1 to 7.3 show the games played by True Believers, Complacent Opponents, and Reluctant Terrorists.

The game is one of incomplete and imperfect information, and so it starts with a move by nature. The type of incomplete information faced by the group is that the group does not know if it is facing a responsive or a nasty government. We write that with probability p, the government is a responsive type and with probability $1 - p$, it is nasty.

The choice faced by the group is whether to commit an act of terrorist violence or to request a concession from the government that will satisfy the group politically.

If the group chooses violence, the game ends with a "terrorist act" outcome that leads to no cooperative negotiations and no change in government position.

If the group requests a concession from the government (making its claims public and perhaps asking for a commission to investigate its complaints or start some kind of negotiation), then the government must decide how to respond. The government can either repress the group or negotiate with it, leading to either a "repression" or "good-faith negotiation" outcome.

The payoffs for each outcome are listed as (group payoff, government payoff).

a) Solve the True Believers game using backwards induction in Figure 7.1; show your work on the figure. What is the outcome if the government is expected to be responsive? What is the outcome if the government is expected to be nasty? Does the government's type matter? Why or why not?

_____

_____

_____

_____

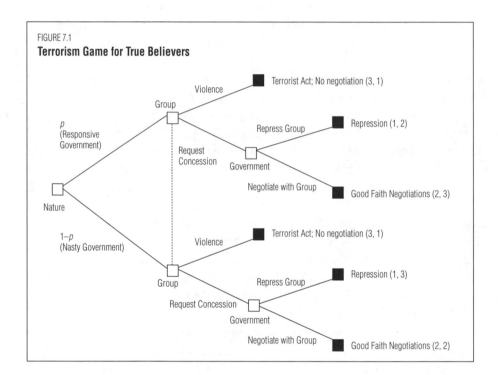

FIGURE 7.1
Terrorism Game for True Believers

b) Solve the Complacent Opponents game using backwards induction in Figure 7.2; show your work on the figure. What is the outcome if the government is expected to be responsive? What is the outcome if the government is expected to be nasty? Does the government's type matter? Why or why not?

_____

_____

_____

_____

c) Solve the Reluctant Terrorists game using backwards induction in Figure 7.3; show your work on the figure. What is the outcome if the government is expected to be responsive? What is the outcome if the government is expected to be nasty? Does the government's type matter? Why or why not?

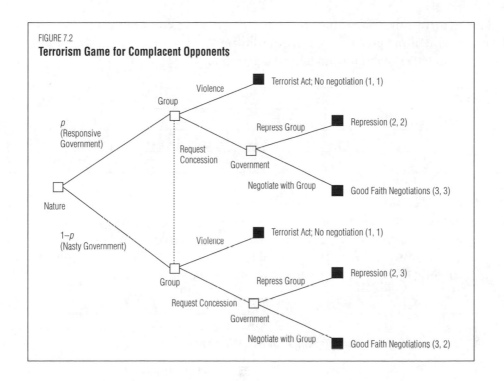

FIGURE 7.2
Terrorism Game for Complacent Opponents

FIGURE 7.3
Terrorism Game for Reluctant Terrorists

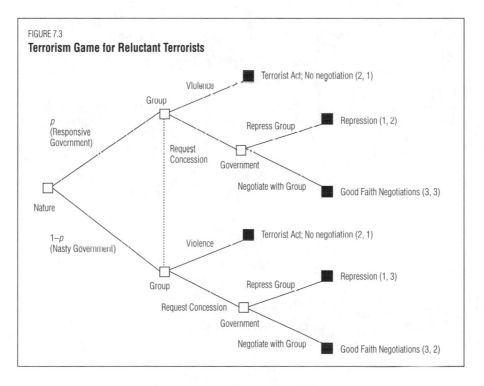

d) The reluctant terrorist game shows that violence can occur in a country because of mistaken perceptions and not just because of the presence of fanatics who are set on a violent path. Using insights gained from Figure 7.3, how can violence result from mistaken perceptions?

_____

_____

_____

_____

_____

Evaluating the Terrorists' Choices

As in our previous games of uncertainty, what is critical in the Reluctant Terrorist game is the potential terrorists' belief about the opponent (here, the government) that they face. We can compute how certain the reluctant terrorists must be to request a concession. To do this, we need to use cardinal payoffs. These payoffs are that $U_{terrorist\ act} = 0.4$, that $U_{repression} = 0$, and $U_{negotiations} = 1$. The group will request a concession if $EU_{request\ concession} > EU_{violence}$.

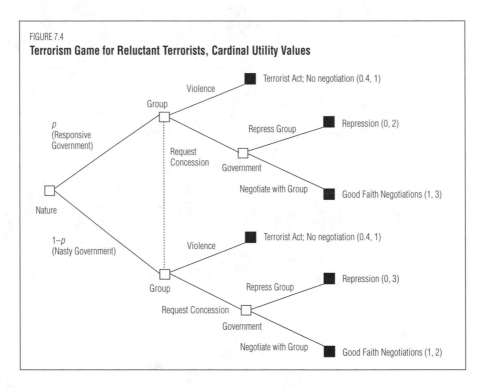

FIGURE 7.4
Terrorism Game for Reluctant Terrorists, Cardinal Utility Values

e) Write the expression for $EU_{request\ concession}$ in general form (that is, as a formula with no payoffs in it) and then substitute the cardinal utilities. Simplify the expression as much as possible.

f) Write the expression for $EU_{violence}$ (Note: this is equal to $U_{terrorist\ act}$) in general form and then substitute the cardinal utilities. Simplify the expression as much as possible.

g) Compute the critical value p for which the group will request a concession. What does that value mean? Explain the answer you found.

_____

_____

_____

Exercise 7-2. _Terrorism and Credible Commitment_

a) Why might a government have difficulty making a credible commitment to terrorists about concessions or negotiations? How does the presence of multiple groups of terrorists help to mitigate this problem?

_____

_____

_____

_____

b) Why might a group of moderates (reluctant terrorists) have difficulty making a credible commitment to the government about restraining any hardliner groups?

_____

_____

_____

_____

c) What incentives do the moderates have to exaggerate their control over the hardliners? What incentives do the moderates have to understate their control over the hardliners?

_____

_____

_____

_____

d) Considering your answer to part c of this exercise, how might the government try to determine the true level of control that the moderates have? What kinds of things could it do, ask the moderates to do, or look for to help it discover the actual extent of the moderates' control? Identify two or three of these screening techniques—that is, actions that one party can take to compel another to reveal its private information (here, its type) truthfully that the government might use or separating moves that the government might seek.

_____

_____

_____

_____

Exercise 7-3. *A Simultaneous Model of Terrorism*

The game below depicts an interaction between a government and a group of potential terrorists. In this game, the government may choose one of three moves: do nothing, install passive deterrence measures (like metal detectors at shopping malls and bomb-sniffing dogs on buses), or take active measures (typically, targeting the terrorists with military or special forces attacks). The terrorists can choose from two moves, do nothing or attack. These moves are interdependent because the government's choice of counterterror strategy influences the cost and, likely, success rate (that is to say, the terrorists' expected utility) of violence.

We assume here that the government's move is concealed from the potential terrorists; the potential terrorists do not have complete intelligence on the government's use of its counterterror funds, and so they do not know whether the government has chosen to acquire passive defenses or whether it has prepared an active response. This assumption allows us to model the situation as the simultaneous-move strategic form game shown in Table 7.1.

TABLE 7.1

Terrorism Game I

		Government		
		Do Nothing	**Passive Measures**	**Active Measures**
Potential Terrorists	**Not Attack**	0, 10	–6, –1	–12, –10
	Attack	10, –10	4, 3	–5, –5

We assume as well that active measures are both more expensive than passive measures and more likely to deter or thwart an attack. Note that the game uses cardinal utilities; some values are negative.

a) Solve this game as we have before. For each of the column player's choices, the row player asks which of her moves makes her best off. For each of the row player's choices, the column player asks which of his moves makes him best off. What, if any, is the equilibrium or equilibria? Show your work, and circle the equilibrium in the table.

Expanding the Game

The previous game allowed the potential terrorists two moves, do nothing or attack. Let's see now what happens to the game when the terrorists' moves become more complex: they now can choose among doing nothing, staging a small attack, and staging a large attack.

The government spends resources needlessly if it takes active measures against a group that prefers to do nothing. Taking active measures against a small attack is costly but eliminates a future threat. Taking active measures against a large attack is costly, and the attack itself will have some costs.

TABLE 7.2

Terrorism Game II

		Government		
		Do Nothing	**Passive Measures**	**Active Measures**
Potential Terrorists	**Not Attack**	0, 10	–6, –1	–12, –10
	Small Attack	7, –4	–8, –6	–11, –7
	Large Attack	12, –11	9, –8	–10, –9

b) Solve this game as before; please show your work in the table. (*Hint:* We solve this game the same way we did the 2 × 2s and the 2 × 3 above. For each of the column player's choices, the row player asks which of her moves makes her best off. For each of the row player's choices, the column player asks which of his moves makes him best off.) What, if any, is the equilibrium or equilibria?

_____

_____

c) Which player has a dominant strategy? Considering the reasoning behind the other actor's preferences, why does this make sense?

_____

_____

d) Describe the preferred strategy of the player who does not have a dominant strategy. Does this player use all of his or her strategies? If yes, under which conditions (against which opponent move) is each used? If not, which strategy is dominated? (A dominated strategy is one that is never a best response to any move by the opponent.)

_____

_____

_____

e) Compare the games in Tables 7.1 and 7.2. What is the effect of adding the third move for the terrorists? In other words, how do our predicted choices and expected outcome differ across the two games?

_____

_____

_____

When Will the Government Take Active Measures?

f) In part d of this exercise, you should have found that the government will <u>never take active measures</u>. Why? Consider the government's payoffs and justify the preference ordering that makes it prefer passive measures even if faced with a large attack.

_____

_____

_____

_____

g) *Challenge:* Devise and justify a payoff ordering in which the government prefers to take active measures. Show your revised game and its solution, and your justification, on a separate sheet of paper.

h) *Challenge:* Changing the government's payoffs is not the only way to arrive at outcomes in which the government prefers to take active measures. Use the original government payoffs given in Table 7.2, but now devise and justify a payoff ordering for the potential terrorists that results in the government preferring to take active measures. Show your revised game and its solution, and your justification, on a separate sheet of paper.

CHAPTER 8

MILITARY INTERVENTION AND DEMOCRATIZATION

EXPLORING THE OUTCOMES OF INTERVENTION

Exercise 8-1. *Reviewing the Argument*

a) Give two examples of leaders who were removed from office by a foreign power after experiencing military defeat at the hands of that power. Use cases other than Germany or Japan after World War II or Iraq and Afghanistan in the 2000s.

_____

_____

b) What type of government did the victor advocate or install in each case in which the defeated state's leader was deposed? Characterize the new governments in terms of their values on W and S; use our regular coding scheme of small, medium, and large.

_____

_____

c) Give two examples of states, other than Iraq and Afghanistan, that experienced a military intervention that led to the creation of a new government or constitution in the occupied/intervened-in state.

_____

_____

d) What type of government did the occupier/intervener advocate or install in each case? Characterize the new governments in terms of their values on *W* and *S*; use our regular coding scheme of small, medium, and large.

_____

_____

e) Why is installing a democracy (large winning coalition system) in defeated or occupied states not in the interests of the outside power? Identify the type of system the outside or intervening power most prefers and explain why.

_____

_____

_____

_____

f) Why might a democratic state choose to install a democratic government anyway? How likely is this to happen? Link your answer to the interests of leaders.

_____

_____

_____

Exercise 8-2.   *Comparing Postwar Germany and Austria*

At the end of World War II, the four victorious powers occupied Germany and Japan. This fact is widely known. Lesser known, though, is the quadripartite occupation of Austria, which was also considered to be a primary belligerent in the war. Much as they did in Germany, the four Allied powers divided Austria and its capital, Vienna, into occupation zones. In Germany, this process was tense, and the Soviets often refused to cooperate with the other zones even on everyday matters such as postal service. Ultimately, the three western zones of Germany merged in 1949 and became the (democratic) Federal Republic of Germany. The Soviet zone remained separate and became the German Democratic Republic (Communist East Germany). The hardening of this division is seen by many as one of the first events of the cold war. Foreign forces remained in both states, and the occupiers continued to exert influence over the foreign policies of both Germanys (though much less so in the West).

In Austria, however, events evolved very differently. Cooperation between the four occupying powers was smooth and effective. By the late 1940s and early 1950s, a coherent national political system existed, and the Austrians began choosing their own leaders to work with the occupying powers. In 1955, the Austrians and the occupiers signed the Austrian State Treaty. The treaty committed Austria to remaining neutral in the emerging cold war, and Austria declared that it would refrain from joining any alliances. It also created a democratic, multi-party political system and a largely free-market economy. The signing of this treaty ended the occupation and removed all foreign troops from Austria.

The puzzle of the Austrian case is this: Austria and Germany are about as similar as we can possibly hope for on many potential independent variables: educated populations, prior experience with democracy and capitalism, religious and ethnic heritage, geographic region, nature of the nondemocratic interregnum, purpose of the intervention/occupation, identity of occupiers (and, subsequently, the size and composition of their winning coalitions and selectorates), acceptance of Marshall Plan aid, etc. We couldn't ask for a closer pair for a natural experiment. We know, though, that we can't explain variables that differ across cases—the outcomes of occupier cooperation and unification—with constants (variables that are the same across cases). If all of these independent variables are constant across the two cases, what explains the variation on outcomes?

a) Propose a hypothesis to explain the variation in occupier cooperation. Indicate your proposed independent variable on the line to the right of the hypothesis, and put an up or down arrow in front of it to indicate whether increasing or decreasing your dependent variable would result in increased occupier cooperation. Then briefly explain the theory behind your hypothesis: Why do you think your proposed independent variable explains the variation in outcomes between the two cases? (*Hint:* You might want to do a bit of research to verify that your variable differs between the two cases.)

$\uparrow$ occupier cooperation $\leftarrow$ _____

_____

_____

_____

_____

b) Propose a hypothesis to explain the variation in post-occupation unification. Indicate your proposed independent variable on the line to the right of the hypothesis, and put an up or down arrow in front of it to indicate whether increasing or decreasing your dependent variable would result in complete unification after occupation. Then briefly explain the theory behind your hypothesis: Why do you think your proposed independent variable explains the variation in outcomes between the two cases? (*Hint:* Again, you might want to do a bit of research to verify that your variable differs between the two cases.)

↑ post-occupation unification ← _____

_____

_____

_____

_____

c) For one of your hypotheses, briefly identify one type of evidence that would support your argument and one type of evidence that would falsify it. (*Hint:* What types of things—actions, thoughts in official memos or documents, things reported in the newspapers—would you expect to observe if your argument were right, and what would you expect to observe if it were wrong?)

_____

_____

_____

_____

Exercise 8-3. *Comparing Interventions*

In this exercise, you'll explore and compare two interventions. What did the intervener want—what was its motivation for the intervention? Was it successful at achieving its goals? If not, why not? What kind of political system did the intervener (want to) install in the target state?

Choose one case from each column to complete Table 8.1 below. Be sure to pick two cases from the same era— either cold war (1946–1990) or post–cold war (1991–present).

Soviet Union – Afghanistan 1979	United States – Grenada 1983
Vietnam – Cambodia 1971	Belgium – Congo 1960
Iraq – Kuwait 1990	US/UN coalition – Kuwait 1991
USSR – Czechoslovakia 1968	South Africa – Lesotho 1998

Code questions about *W*, *S*, Executive Recruitment, and Democracy Summary as in Exercise 6-4.

The Data

- Intervener Goals – What were the intervener's public goals or stated motivations for the intervention? You may wish to note if sources indicate a significant divergence between public rhetoric and underlying intentions.
- Successful Intervention – Did the intervention achieve the stated goals? Code this as full, partial, none, or regression. "Regression" in this context refers to a post-intervention status quo that is worse for the intervener than the pre-intervention status quo. This may be an appropriate code, for example, when the attempted intervention was met with force and was repelled, and the target country then attacked the intervener in response.
- Intervener's Preferred Regime Type – Note here if the intervener made any explicit claims or statements about its preferred post-intervention regime in the target state. If you find no evidence of explicitly stated preferences, code this variable as 0. If explicit claims occurred, code this variable as 1 and note the content of the claims.
- Post-intervention Regime Type – Characterize the post-intervention regime in terms of the size of its *W* and *S*, both of which are coded as small, medium, or large. Note significant changes, if any, to each from the pre-intervention regime.

TABLE 8.1
Comparing Interventions

	Case 1: _____	Case 2: _____
Era		
Intervener Political Institutions:		
a) Who is in S?		
b) How big is s?		
c) Who is in W?		
d) How big is W?		
Executives:		
e) Who is the leader?		
f) How did the leader attain office?		
g) Democracy Summary		
Target:		
h) How did the leader attain office?		
i) Democracy Summary		
Intervener Motivation:		
j) Intervener Goals		
k) Successful Intervention?		
Dependent Variable:		
l) Hypothesized Regime Type		
m) Intervener's Preferred Regime Type		
n) Post-intervention Regime Type		

Comparing the Cases

o) The two lists contain autocratic and democratic interveners, respectively. According to the theory presented in Chapter 8, what types of goals should we expect for democratic interveners? What kind of goals should we expect for autocratic interveners?

_____

_____

_____

p) In each case, did the intervening state achieve its goals? If you coded success as yes, briefly describe the evidence to support that coding. If you coded success as no, briefly speculate on why the intervener was unable to achieve its goals.

_____

_____

_____

_____

q) Did the observed post-intervention regime (or intervener regime preferences) match the hypothesized post-intervention regime (or regime preference)? How well does the theory seem to fit the two cases you investigated?

_____

_____

_____

r) This exercise asked you to pick two cases from the same era, either cold war or post–cold war. By doing so, we control for that variable—that is to say, hold it constant across cases. As we reviewed in Exercise 8-2 above, we cannot explain a variable (like the different outcomes we observe across the cases) with a constant. Controlling for era allows us to ensure that any difference in outcomes is actually caused by something else—hopefully, our independent variable of interest.

Let's problematize that assumption, that era is a potential causal variable. Does the theory presented in *Principles* give any reason to believe that the era will matter? Explain your answer: How might era affect our dependent variable, and why might we expect no effect? Do you think we need to control for era here? Why or why not? What other important variables do you think we *should* control in a comparison like this? For one proposed control variable, briefly explain your rationale for why it might influence the outcome (and thus should be controlled).

_____

_____

_____

_____

_____

_____

_____

CHAPTER 9

WHAT'S THE PROBLEM WITH FOREIGN AID?

INVESTIGATING FOREIGN AID

Exercise 9-1. *The Problems of World Politics and the Problems of Foreign Aid*

Chapter 3 presented four problems of world politics—coordination, distribution, monitoring, and sanctioning—and asserted that these four problems describe a wide range of behaviors in international relations. This exercise asks you to locate examples (or potential examples) of each of these problems in the politics of foreign aid.

Donors and Recipients

Consider the game played by a potential donor of foreign aid and a potential recipient. Identify an example of each of the problems of world politics in this interaction.

a) Coordination:

> *Example Answer: Donors and recipients need to coordinate on which projects to fund so that the donor isn't giving money for projects the recipient can't do or doesn't want.*

b) Distribution:

c) Monitoring:

d) Sanctioning:

Between Donors

About thirty different states (and a number of multilateral organizations) give aid. Consider now the game played between donors.

e) Coordination:

   Example Answer: Donors want to coordinate on a plan for funding projects so that they don't fund the same project twice or fund projects that work against one another. These situations waste resources.

   _____

   _____

   _____

   _____

f) Distribution:

   _____

   _____

   _____

   _____

g) Monitoring:

   _____

   _____

   _____

   _____

h) Sanctioning:

   _____

   _____

   _____

   _____

Exercise 9-2.   *Comparing Aid Programs*

   In 2002, U.S. president George W. Bush announced a new way of allocating a significant part of U.S. foreign aid (known as official development assistance, ODA, in policy circles). He proposed to distribute aid as grants to countries that committed themselves to principles of good governance (such as transparency, reduced corruption, and rule of law), democracy, human capital development, and market principles. Under this Millennium Challenge Program, potential recipients can propose a project, and the level of funding available to that state is conditional on the state's governance. You can read more about the Program at www.mcc.gov.

The Data

Consider *Principles*'s discussions of the Marshall Plan and of traditional ODA programs, and compare them to the Millennium Challenge Program by completing Table 9.1.

TABLE 9.1

Comparing Aid Programs

	Traditional ODA	**Marshall Plan**	**Millennium Challenge Program**
a) Amount Allocated*	$11.9 billion	$13.2 billion over four years	$2.2 billion
b) Program Motivation(s) or Objective(s)			
c) Types of Projects Funded			
d) Program Administering Agency			
e) Recipient Selection Process			
f) Major Recipients			
g) Key Characteristics of Major Recipients			

* Fiscal Year 2007 for ODA and MCP; Marshall Plan adjusted for inflation to FY 2007 dollars.

Comparing the Cases

h) What characteristics does the Millennium Challenge Program share with traditional ODA programs? What characteristics does it share with the Marshall Plan?

_____

_____

_____

i)   What are some key differences between the Millennium Challenge Program and traditional ODA programs and between the Program and the Marshall Plan?

_____

_____

_____

_____

j)   Consider the program's primary, or major, recipients of aid and the hypotheses about recipients presented in Table 9.1 of *Principles*. Do these cases support that hypotheses? Indicate which cases do and which cases do not support the hypotheses, and briefly propose an explanation for the anomalous (mispredicted) cases. (*Hint:* You might need to do a bit of research on the winning coalition and selectorate size for these countries.)

_____

_____

_____

_____

_____

_____

k)   Consider the Millennium Challenge Program's method for choosing recipients and aid levels. How does such an approach serve U.S. interests? Does this approach serve U.S. interests better or worse than traditional approaches? Justify your response.

_____

_____

_____

_____

l)   How successful is ODA at achieving its objectives, and why? How successful was the Marshall Plan at achieving its objectives, and why? Based on the similarities and differences you identified above, how likely do you think the Millennium Challenge Program will be at achieving its objectives? Explain why.

_____

_____

_____

_____

_____

_____

Exercise 9-3.   *Grant, Loans, and Foreign Aid*

Only a small amount of foreign aid—estimates suggest about 10%—is given directly to recipients as a no-strings-attached gift. The vast majority of ODA is in the form of loans. The loans are usually at concessionary interest rates, with the interest rate on the loan set below market levels and the donor subsidizing the difference between the market rate and the loan rate. The recipient state, however, is still obligated to pay back the loans, and even at the low interest rate and with a generous repayment period, this can result in a significant burden for a developing economy.

Why Use Loans?

a) Why might states use loans as foreign aid instead of grants? Present and justify two hypotheses for why states would choose to give loans as foreign aid. (*Hint:* What is your dependent variable here?)

_____

_____

_____

_____

b) Why do some states get loans and others get grants? Present and justify two hypotheses for why a state might get a grant instead of a loan. Consider characteristics of the recipient state as part of your answer.

_____

_____

_____

_____

Paying It Back

Most foreign aid is used for projects that do not have immediate economic benefits—education, transportation infrastructure, health care, and other public goods. The absence or low levels of return on these investments mean that paying back loans used to fund them is very difficult.[1] Over the last several decades, this has resulted in a crushing level of debt for many poor countries. Most of their export earnings go toward paying down their debt, leaving very little to be invested at home for development. A number of states have defaulted on (ceased to pay) their debts at various times; others have frequently restructured their debts to try to make payments more manageable. Most loans-in-aid are actually loans from major commercial banks, meaning that these private sector entities (and not the governments "giving" the aid) are the ones who lose money when an indebted state defaults.

c) Use the Internet to locate information about the World Bank's Heavily Indebted Poor Countries (HIPC) initiative. On what basis does this program propose to reduce developing country debt—what characteristics or behaviors make a state eligible for relief? How much debt relief can a state get, and how is that relief structured? Identify at least one advantage and one disadvantage to donors of this approach to debt relief.

_____

_____

_____

_____

d) How well does the design of this program fit with the theory of foreign aid presented in Chapter 9? Explain your response.

_____

_____

_____

_____

---

[1] A significant amount is pocketed by unscrupulous and corrupt leaders; the effect on national income is the same.

e) Use the Internet to locate information about the Jubilee 2000 campaign. How does this program's approach to debt relief differ from that of the HIPC? Identify at least one advantage and one disadvantage to donors of the Jubilee 2000 approach to debt relief.

_____

_____

_____

_____

_____

f) How well does the design of the Jubilee 2000 program fit with the theory of foreign aid presented in Chapter 9? Explain your response.

_____

_____

_____

_____

Exercise 9-4. *The Puzzle of Multilateral Aid*

The argument for foreign aid presented in *Principles* revolves around the goal of obtaining policy concessions in a bilateral (two-state) relationship. A new puzzle arises, then, when considering the 30% of ODA that states distribute through multilateral organizations like the World Bank and the European Union. By definition, that aid is distributed through the organization and is not subject to the decision-making processes or interests of the original state donor.

a) Why might states choose to give aid through multilateral organizations? Explain at least two reasons why states would choose to donate through an organization rather than donate directly to a recipient.

_____

_____

_____

_____

b) Hypothesize about the relationship between multilateral ODA and development outcomes. Should we expect multilateral aid to produce more growth (or poverty alleviation) than bilateral aid, or would it produce the same amount or less growth? Explain the logic behind your hypothesis.

_____

_____

_____

_____

_____

Exercise 9-5. *Comparing Aid Recipients*

Recipients of ODA vary greatly in their degree of economic and social need, their degree of democracy, and also their degree of interest to outside donors. This exercise asks you to collect information about three countries and test them against those three hypotheses of aid receipts.

The Data

Select one case from each column. Use the coding rules below to complete Table 9.2 for your selected cases. As before, most of the data is available from the CIA World Fact Book (www.cia.gov/library/publications/the-world-factbook)

TABLE 9.2

Comparing Aid Recipients

	Case 1: _____	Case 2: _____	Case 3: _____
Independent Variables: Poverty:			
a) Region			
b) Income Classification			
c) Poverty			
d) Infant Mortality			
e) Literacy			
Democracy:			
f) Size of W (key member groups)			
g) Size of S (key member groups)			
h) Executive Recruitment			
i) Democracy Summary			
Donor Interests:			
j) Largest Donor			
k) Strategic Interests			
Dependent Variable:			
l) Total Foreign Aid			

or the Country Pages/Profiles of the British Foreign and Commonwealth Office (www.fco.gov.uk) or the U.S. Department of State (www.state.gov); additional data on foreign aid is available from the Organization for Economic Cooperation and Development at http://stats.oecd.org/qwids/. For each piece of data, please indicate the year that data reflects (i.e., a 2008 estimate of poverty, a 2006 estimate of primary education, etc.). You should use the most recent available data.

Libya	Lebanon	Bangladesh
North Korea	Haiti	Turkey
Syria	Belarus	Malawi
Cuba	Tanzania	Nicaragua
Turkmenistan	Pakistan	Palestinian Authority

- Income Classification: Use the World Bank's classifications of upper middle income, lower middle income, and low income. These are available from the World Bank, www.worldbank.org.
- Poverty T: Percentage of the country's population living at or below the World Bank's poverty threshold of USD 2 per day.
- Infant mortality: Death rate among children younger than 5 years of age.
- Literacy: Percentage of the country's population able to read at an eighth-grade level.
- Size of W: Small, medium, large. Include a brief list of key societal groups (military, single party members, small business owners, urban labor, etc.) supporting the leader.
- Size of S: Small, medium, large. Include a brief description of what societal groups are members of S.
- Executive Recruitment: Selection or election. See Exercise 6-4 for the definitions of these terms.

- Total Foreign Aid: Total aid (grants and loans) received from all sources. This data is available from U.S Overseas Loans and Grants Greenbook at http://qesdb.cdie.org/gbk/index.html.
- Major Donor: Identify the actor that provides the largest share (as a percentage of total aid) of the recipient's aid. This may be an international organization such as the World Bank or European Union. This data is available from the US Agency for International Development (USAID) at www.usaid.gov/pubs/cbj2002/index.html.
- Strategic Interests: Weak, moderate, strong. Briefly identify any strategic or other key interests that the donor has in the recipient.
- Democracy Summary: Overall assessment of democracy level based on *W, S,* and Executive Recruitment. Code this variable as in Exercise 6-4.

Comparing the Cases

m) Consider your data on need, as indicated in rows b-e. Does higher need appear to be related to higher total aid? (*Hint:* Rank your cases in order of need. Then rank them by total aid. Do the lists match?) Describe the relationship you find: Is it positive or negative? How strong is the relationship?

_____

_____

_____

n) Consider your data on democracy, as indicated in row i. Does more democracy appear to be related to higher total aid? Describe the relationship you find: Is it positive or negative? How strong is the relationship?

_____

_____

_____

o) Consider your data on donor interests, as indicated in row k. Do donor interests appear to be related to higher total aid? Describe the relationship you find: Is it positive or negative? How strong is the relationship?

_____

_____

_____

p) Compare your responses to parts m, n, and o of this exercise. Which of the three competing hypotheses— need, democracy, or interests—does the best job of explaining the pattern of outcomes that you found? Explain your answer.

_____

_____

_____

_____

CHAPTER 10

THE INTERNATIONAL POLITICAL ECONOMY OF TRADE

COMPARATIVE ADVANTAGE AND TRADE

Exercise 10-1. *Free Trade in Widgets and Gizmos*
  The following table indicates the productivity (the amount of output produced by one worker per day) of two countries (Malistan and Ukralia) for two particular goods (widgets and gizmos). Assume these are the only two countries that can trade these items with each other. Answer the questions below using this table.

a) Which country has an absolute advantage in producing widgets?

b) Which country has an absolute advantage in producing gizmos?

TABLE 10.1

Free Trade in Widgets and Gizmos

	Malistan	Ukralia
widget	8 widgets/day	6 widgets/day
gizmo	10 gizmos/day	20 gizmos/day

c) Which country has a comparative advantage in producing widgets?

d) Which country has a comparative advantage in producing gizmos?

e) Under free trade, which country would produce widgets?

f) Under free trade, which country would produce gizmos?

Exercise 10-2. *Free Trade in Bells and Whistles*
  The following table indicates the productivity (the amount of output produced by one worker per day) of two other countries, Zaioff and Lundikistan, for two particular goods (bells and whistles). Assume these are the only two countries that can trade these items with each other. Answer the questions below using this table.

TABLE 10.2

Free Trade in Bells and Whistles

	Zaioff	Lundikistan
bell	8 bells/day	4 bells/day
whistle	12 whistles/day	4 whistles/day

a) Which country has an absolute advantage in producing bells?

b) Which country has an absolute advantage in producing whistles?

c) Which country has a comparative advantage in producing bells?

_____

d) Which country has a comparative advantage in producing whistles?

_____

e) Under free trade, which country would produce bells?

_____

f) Under free trade, which country would produce whistles?

_____

Exercise 10-3. *Trade Restrictions I*

Assume that the United States and Germany are trading partners. Assume further that in some year Germany exported 100,000 cars to the United States at a price of $30,000 (U.S.) each. But then the United States placed a quota on imported cars from Germany, limiting the number to 75,000 per year.

a) What happens to the price of German cars in the United States? Why?

_____

_____

b) What happens to the volume of imported cars from Germany? Why?

_____

_____

c) What happens to sales of domestic cars in the United States? Why?

_____

_____

d) Who in the United States is hurt by this decision? Why?

_____

_____

e) Who in the United States benefits from this decision? Why?

_____

_____

f) Who in Germany is hurt by this decision? Why?

_____

_____

Exercise 10-4. *Trade Restrictions II*

Assume that the United States and Germany are trading partners. Assume further that in some year Germany exported 100,000 cars to the United States at a price of $30,000 (U.S.) each. But then the United States places a 10 percent tariff on cars imported from Germany.

a) What happens to the price of German cars in the United States? Why?

_____

_____

b) What happens to the volume of imported cars from Germany? Why?

_____

_____

c) What happens to sales of domestic cars in the United States? Why?

_____

_____

Exercise 10-5. *Exchange Rates I*

You are a banker watching exchange rates between the United States and Norway. In June 2007, one United States dollar was equal to 5.86 Norwegian kroner. You look again in July 2008 and see that one U.S. dollar is now equal to 5.64 kroner.

a) Has the krone gotten stronger or weaker against the dollar?

_____

_____

b) Has the dollar gotten stronger or weaker against the krone?

_____

_____

c) Given your answers to parts a and b of this exercise, will this result in Norway importing more or fewer goods from the United States? Why?

_____

_____

d) Who in the United States benefits from the new exchange rate? Why?

_____

_____

e) Who in the United States is hurt by the new exchange rate? Why?

_____

_____

Exercise 10-6. *Exchange Rates II*

Now you are a banker watching exchange rates between the United States and South Korea. In June 2008, one U.S. dollar was equal to 1,225 South Korean won. You look again in June 2009 and see that one U.S. dollar is now equal to 1,400 won.

a) Has the won gotten stronger or weaker against the dollar?

_____

_____

b) Has the dollar gotten stronger or weaker against the won?

_____

_____

c) Given your answers to parts a and b of this exercise, will the shift in exchange rates result in South Korea exporting more or fewer goods to the United States? Why?

_____

_____

_____

d) Who in the United States benefits from the new exchange rate? Why?

_____

_____

e) Who in the United States is hurt by the new exchange rate? Why?

_____

_____

Exercise 10-7.   *U.S.-Japanese Trade Restrictions*

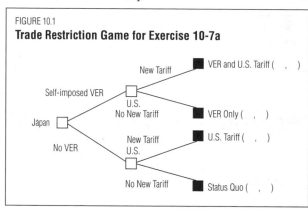

FIGURE 10.1
Trade Restriction Game for Exercise 10-7a

New Tariff — VER and U.S. Tariff (,)

Self-imposed VER

U.S.
No New Tariff — VER Only (,)

Japan

New Tariff
U.S. — U.S. Tariff (,)

No VER

No New Tariff — Status Quo (,)

Japan and the United States get into arguments over trade on a regular basis, with the United States typically accusing Japan of unfair trade practices and threatening to impose trade barriers to the sale of Japanese products (mostly cars and electronics) in the United States. Figure 10.1 depicts a trade restriction game between the two countries. This game represents a situation in which the U.S. Congress has threatened to impose new tariffs on Japan to slow the import of Japanese cars into the United States. Japan is also considering placing a Voluntary Export Restriction (VER) on its exports. If Japan places a voluntary export restriction on its products, it will voluntarily cut back shipments to the United States. If the United States places a tariff on Japanese imports, it will make Japanese cars more expensive, also resulting in lower shipments of Japanese cars to the United States.

Japan would most prefer to export freely to the United States, with no restrictions, either voluntary or imposed. The least-preferred option for the Japanese is to place a voluntary restriction on their exports and also have the United States impose additional tariffs. But if some kind of restriction is going to be imposed, the Japanese would rather hold back their own exports (using a VER) than be embarrassed when the U.S. Congress publicly announces that Japan is not trading fairly. Japan would also have more control over a self-imposed VER than over a new complicated trade law written by Congress. So for Japan, the payoff ordering is:

Status Quo > VER only > U.S. Tariff > VER and U.S. Tariff

For the U.S. Congress, the least-preferred outcome is to do nothing and allow continued unlimited Japanese exports into the United States, because members of Congress and the president are facing domestic pressure to do something about the loss of U.S. jobs to overseas markets. So the status quo is unacceptable and is the worst possible outcome. At the same time, although the Congress would like to place some trade restrictions on Japan, it does not want to totally cut off the flow of goods from Japan into the United States. So the combination of a VER and additional tariffs is the second-worst outcome. When it comes to a choice of restrictions between a VER and a tariff, assume that Congress would prefer the political statement of imposing a tariff on Japan—this is the best outcome from Congress's point of view. The second-best outcome is for Japan to impose a VER, while Congress holds off on tariffs (this is still much better than having the Japanese continue to export unlimited quantities of goods to the United States).

U.S. Tariff > VER only > VER and U.S. Tariff > Status Quo

a) Write the preferences for Japan and a punitive Congress in the game in Figure 10.1.

b) Solve the game in Figure 10.1 by backwards induction. Write the complete equilibrium.

Changing the U.S.'s Preferences

Assume now that the U.S. Congress's preferences change.

For Japan: Assume Japanese preferences remain the same as in Exercise 10-7.

For the United States: Assume that Congress does not care if it totally cuts off trade with Japan and that it wants to punish Japan as much as possible for (perceived) trade violations in the past. For this vengeful Congress, the combination of a VER and additional tariffs is the best possible outcome. The second-best outcome would be a U.S. tariff, while the Japanese do nothing; the third-best outcome would be a Japanese VER with no U.S. tariff; and the worst outcome would again be to do nothing and allow continued unlimited Japanese exports into the United States. So:

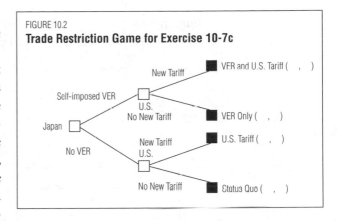

FIGURE 10.2
Trade Restriction Game for Exercise 10-7c

VER and U.S. Tariff > U.S. Tariff > VER only > Status Quo

c) Write the preferences for Japan and the vengeful Congress in the game in Figure 10.2.

d) Solve the game in Figure 10.2 by backwards induction. Write the complete equilibrium.

Comparing the Games

e) Compare the games you drew in Figures 10.1 and 10.2. How do their equilibria differ? Which actors would choose the same moves, and which would choose different ones?

f) You're a Japanese policymaker, and you need to decide whether to adopt a VER. What kinds of evidence might convince you that this U.S. Congress is really of the punitive type and not the vengeful type? Be specific. What information would be convincing and why?

EXTENSIONS

Exercise 10-8.   *Invested Interests*

   Using your college's or university's library resources, obtain a copy of Jeffry A. Frieden's article, "Invested Interests: The Politics of National Economic Policies in a World of Global Finance," from *International Organization* 45, 4 (Autumn 1991): 525–551. Skim the article, then use that information to help you determine where to read more closely to answer these questions.

a) What are the three Mundell-Fleming conditions? How many can a state have at the same time?

_____

_____

_____

b) What effect of capital mobility causes Frieden to argue that before capital mobility (BCM) and after capital mobility (ACM) political coalition patterns will differ?

_____

_____

c) What are Frieden's three "realistic and analytically useful" reasons for adopting a specific-factors approach?

_____

_____

_____

d) On what two dimensions of exchange rate policy does Frieden base his predictions?

_____

_____

e) In your own words, explain why "producers of nontradable goods and services" are placed where they are in the predictions table on page 545 of the article. (*Hint:* Your response might draw on the concepts in part a of this exercise.)

_____

_____

_____

_____

f) All of Frieden's examples are drawn from the developed world. Consider the interests of domestic groups in a capital-poor country. Do Frieden's predictions for interests in the ACM world seem reasonable in such a situation? Briefly explain why or why not.

_____

_____

_____

_____

_____

CHAPTER 11

INTERNATIONAL ORGANIZATIONS AND INTERNATIONAL LAW

THE USEFULNESS OF INTERNATIONAL REGIMES

In Exercises 11-1 through 11-4, assume that you are trying to achieve mutually beneficial (cooperative) outcomes in the corresponding game. In some of these games, an international regime is necessary or helpful for achieving cooperation. In others, it is not. In each game, consider whether a regime can, in fact, help to achieve cooperation, and why or how it can do so. The Online Appendix reviews the ideas of necessary and sufficient conditions.

Exercise 11-1. *The Necessity of Regimes I*

a) See Table 11.1. What is the single-play Nash equilibrium in this game? Write it in equilibrium notation. (*Hint:* See Chapter 3 if you need a refresher.)

TABLE 11.1
Game for Exercise 11-1

A	B	
	Cooperate	**Defect**
Cooperate	(3, 3)	(1, 4)
Defect	(4, 1)	(2, 2)

b) Can mutual cooperation (a CC outcome) ever be achieved in this game (possibly assuming repeated play)? If so, how?

c) Is a regime necessary, helpful, or irrelevant in achieving cooperation in this game, and why?

Exercise 11-2. *The Necessity of Regimes II*

a) See Table 11.2. What is the single-play, pure strategy Nash equilibrium in this game? Write it in equilibrium notation.

TABLE 11.2
Game for Exercise 11-2

A	B	
	Left	**Right**
Left	(4, 3)	(1, 1)
Right	(1, 1)	(3, 4)

b) Can mutual cooperation ever be achieved in this game (possibly assuming repeated play)? If so, how?

c) Is a regime necessary, helpful, or irrelevant in achieving cooperation in this game, and why?

_____

_____

_____

_____

TABLE 11.3

Game for Exercise 11-3

A	B	
	Cooperate	**Defect**
Cooperate	(4, 4)	(3, 2)
Defect	(2, 3)	(1, 1)

Exercise 11-3. *The Necessity of Regimes III*

a) See Table 11.3. What is the single-play Nash equilibrium in this game?

_____

b) Can mutual cooperation ever be achieved in this game (possibly assuming repeated play)? If so, how?

_____

_____

c) Is a regime necessary, helpful, or irrelevant in achieving cooperation in this game, and why?

_____

_____

TABLE 11.4

Game for Exercise 11-4

A	B	
	Cooperate	**Defect**
Cooperate	(2, 2)	(1, 4)
Defect	(4, 1)	(3, 3)

Exercise 11-4. *The Necessity of Regimes IV*

a) See Table 11.4. What is the single-play Nash equilibrium in this game?

_____

b) Can mutual cooperation ever be achieved in this game (possibly assuming repeated play)? If so, how?

_____

_____

c) Is a regime necessary, helpful, or irrelevant in achieving cooperation in this game, and why?

_____

_____

_____

_____

THE CONTENT OF INTERNATIONAL AGREEMENTS

Exercise 11-5. *Why Do States Form Weak International Agreements?*

Sometimes it seems strange that states form weak international agreements and that rules are watered down even before countries vote to join the agreement. Consider the games in Figures 11.1, 11.2, and 11.3. In these games, the United States and United Nations (UN) are coordinating on the formation of a new international agreement.

1) A UN panel first proposes a set of rules.
2) The United States can then accept or reject these rules.

a) If the United States accepts the rules, then they will be established. After establishment of the new rules/organization, if a signatory state (including the United States) violates the rules, then it will suffer a cost, either a reputational cost in the "court of international public opinion" or perhaps even a material cost, if other states react by imposing penalties on it.

b) If the United States does not accept the rules, then no new rules (no new set of international laws) will be established. In these games, the United States has veto power over the final agreement.

This exercise asks you to determine whether an international agreement can be reached, and if so, whether it will be strong or weak.

United States Supports New International Law

Examine Figure 11.1. Assume that the preferences are as follows:

The UN prefers to have any type of agreement to no agreement. Between a strong or a weak agreement, the best outcome for the UN is to establish a strong agreement—that is, one in which the rules are broad and the UN perhaps has deep investigative and enforcement powers. The second-best outcome is a weaker agreement. The worst option is to have no agreement. But if no agreement is going to be the outcome, the UN rules panel would rather have proposed a strong agreement that can be a model for future agreements. So the panel prefers to have a strong treaty rejected to having a weak treaty rejected. It can also make statements against the United States, arguing, for instance, that it developed a model proposal with far reaching implications, but that states like the United States were unwilling to move forward into the modern world. The UN's preferences are:

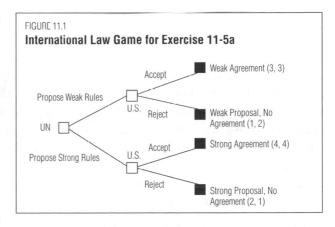

FIGURE 11.1
International Law Game for Exercise 11-5a

Strong agreement > Weak agreement > Strong proposal without agreement > Weak proposal without agreement

In this example, the United States is very supportive of strong international law that is expected to apply to any state, including the United States. The United States prefers to have a strong agreement, with a weak agreement being second best. Unlike the UN, however, the United States would prefer to see a weak treaty rejected rather than a strong one. This would give U.S. leaders the opportunity to take a leadership role in future negotiations, claiming that stronger leadership must be shown in order to achieve an even stronger set of rules that would be accepted.

The preferences of the United States are (as shown in Figure 11.1):

Strong agreement > Weak agreement > Weak proposal without agreement > Strong proposal without agreement

a) Solve the game in Figure 11.1 by backwards induction. Show your work in the figure.

b) What is the outcome of this game? _____

c) What is the equilibrium path for this game? Write it in equilibrium notation. (*Hint:* See Chapter 3 if you need a refresher.) _____

d) What is the full equilibrium for this game? Write it in equilibrium notation. _____

e) Which problem(s) of international relations—coordination, distribution, monitoring, or sanctioning—are present in this game? Which of the problems has the largest effect on the outcome? Explain your answer.

_____

_____

_____

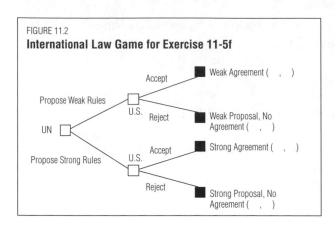

FIGURE 11.2
International Law Game for Exercise 11-5f

United States Reluctant to Support New International Law

In reality, the United States has been reluctant to support strong international agreements that might impinge on U.S. ability to take international action when it deems appropriate. Often, the United States has taken the stance of supporting moderately strong agreements (pushing for some kind of international cooperation, but stopping short of supporting drastic and powerful international organizations and rules). In this case, preferences may be somewhat different.

UN: Assume preferences are identical to before:

Strong agreement > Weak agreement > Strong proposal without agreement > Weak proposal without agreement

Assume that the United States wants some sort of agreement, but not if the agreement is too strong. A strong agreement to which it is subject is the worst outcome. The United States would most prefer signing a sufficiently weak treaty with limited jurisdiction. The second-best option for the United States is to reject a too-strong agreement; it can then claim that the treaty was too large a violation of sovereignty for the United States to accept, and domestic audiences will be sympathetic to this. A weak proposal with rejection by the United States is the third-best option—the United States prefers this to accepting a strong agreement, but it is worse than rejecting a strong agreement, because the administration may be portrayed as unwilling to endorse even modest progress in international law. So for the United States in this case:

Weak agreement > Strong proposal without agreement > Weak proposal without agreement > Strong agreement

f) Solve the game in Figure 11.2 by backwards induction. Show your work in the figure.

g) What is the outcome of this game? _____

h) What is the equilibrium path for this game? Write it in equilibrium notation. _____

i) What is the full equilibrium for this game? Write it in equilibrium notation. _____

j) Which problem(s) of international relations—coordination, distribution, monitoring, or sanctioning—are present in this game? Which of the problems has the largest effect on the outcome? Explain your answer.

_____

_____

_____

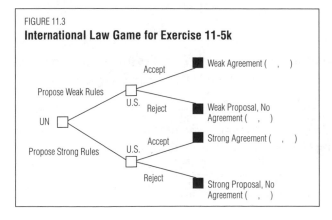

FIGURE 11.3
International Law Game for Exercise 11-5k

United States Opposes New International Law

At times in its history, the United States has refused to accept any limits on its international activity, even minor ones. At these times, any new international agreement has been viewed with suspicion, as any agreement (no matter how innocuous on the surface) can be portrayed as limiting the ability of the United States to do what it believes to be best internationally. In this case, preferences may be somewhat different.

Assume that preferences are:

UN (identical to before):

Strong agreement > Weak agreement > Strong proposal without agreement > Weak proposal without agreement

Assume that the United States refuses to take part in any agreement. A strong agreement to which it is subject is the worst outcome. But agreeing to even a weak treaty is bad; this is the second-worst outcome for the United States. The best option for the United States is to reject a too-strong agreement—U.S. political leaders can then make political hay by claiming that international organizations are clearly out to shackle the United States with agreements that work against U.S. interests. At least some domestic audiences in the United States are expected to be sympathetic to this argument. Rejection of a weak proposal by the United States is the second-best outcome. So for the United States in this case:

Strong proposal without agreement > Weak proposal without agreement > Weak agreement > Strong agreement the

k) Solve the game in Figure 11.3 by backwards induction. Show your work in the figure.

l) What is the outcome of this game? _____

m) What is the equilibrium path for this game? Write it in equilibrium notation. _____

n) What is the full equilibrium for this game? Write it in equilibrium notation. _____

o) Which problem(s) of international relations—coordination, distribution, monitoring, or sanctioning—are present in this game? Which of the problems has the largest effect on the outcome? Explain your answer.

_____

_____

_____

Exercise 11-6. *Commitment, Compliance, and Selection Effects*

Why do states comply with international agreements? States could comply, as constructivist and legalist perspectives suggest, because they feel a moral, legally binding, or other obligation to do so. Other arguments, particularly those associated with the strategic perspective and neorealism, suggest that states comply because the agreement itself contains nothing more than a commitment to do what the states already intended to do.[1] The high level of observed compliance, then, is not a surprise: it is the logical outcome of this selection effect.

These arguments about why states comply also have implications for why states should sign an agreement in the first place. If the constructivist argument is correct, then states' identities should influence joining patterns. For example, states sharing identities should be more likely to behave the same way, with regional geographic identities ("we are African/European/etc.") and idea-based identities ("we are democracies/liberal market economies/etc.") being among the most likely candidates. In this argument, self-identification with a particular group brings with it norms of behavior that good members of that group are expected to follow. The selection effect argument, on the other hand, suggests that we should expect to see states commit to a treaty if they are already in—or nearly in-compliance with the agreement. For a human rights treaty, for example, we would expect that current human rights levels would be a strong predictor of signing the agreement.

Comparing the Arguments: Who Signs?
Tables 11.5, 11.6, 11.7, and 11.8 show data from research on why states sign on to, and then comply with, Article VIII of the International Monetary Fund agreement.[2] States that opt to sign this separate component of the

---

[1] This argument is most closely associated with George Downs, David Rocke, and Peter Barsoom, "Is the Good News about Compliance Good News About Cooperation?" *International Organization* 50, 2 (1996): 269–306.

[2] These data, and the arguments we examine here, are presented in more detail in Beth A. Simmons, "International Law and State Behavior: Commitment and Compliance in International Monetary Affairs." *American Political Science Review* 94, 4 (2000): 819–835, and Jana von Stein, "Do Treaties Constrain or Screen? Selection Bias and Treaty Compliance." *American Political Science Review* 99, 4 (2005): 611–622. We thank the authors for permission to use their data for this exercise.

agreement commit themselves to not placing any restrictions on their current accounts.[3] Compliance with the agreement, then, is "Not Restrict"; defection is "Restrict." Let's begin by looking at the question of who signs.

Table 11.5 explains why states sign Article VIII by examining democracies and nondemocracies. The unit of analysis here—the thing being observed and counted in the cells—is a state-year: one year for a particular state. The scope of analysis is all IMF member states from their year of joining the Fund and all years from 1946 to 1997 for which data were available. The table asks whether democracy (the row, or independent variable) affects an observation's value on Article VIII status (the column, or dependent variable). For this analysis, a state is a democracy if its value on the widely used POLITY IV democracy measurement is greater than or equal to the conventional value of 6 on a scale of −10 to 10. Both of these variables are dichotomous; they can only take on yes-no values. By convention, yes = 1 and no = 0. For this exercise, you will need two highlighters and a calculator.

TABLE 11.5
Article VIII Signing and Democracy

		Article VIII		
		0	**1**	**Total**
Democracy	**0**	1574	447	2021
	1	914	1410	2324
	Total	2488	2857	4345

a) Which school's argument does this table test? _____

b) Eyeball the data. Do the data suggest that being a democracy influences signing? What makes you think this? (*Hint:* What does the theory predict about the values of the cells? What cells do you need to compare to make this inference?)

_____

_____

c) As you'll note from the bottom row of the table, the modal (most frequent) value of "Article VIII" is 0, that is, not signing. Following the standard model of a proportionate reduction in error (PRE) test, the null hypothesis is the most frequent category, not signing. Highlight the cells of Table 11.5 that show correct predictions by the null hypothesis. Then calculate what proportion of the cases the null hypothesis correctly predicts.

d) Using a second highlighter in a different color, indicate which cells are correct predictions by our alternative hypothesis, which democracies are more likely to sign. Then calculate what proportion of the cases the alternative hypothesis correctly predicts.

---

[3]You might think of the current account as a country's checking account—it's the national balance for income (from exports) and debits (imports). Restrictions on the current account might, for example, limit access to foreign exchange to particular individuals, banks, or firms, or they might limit it by quantity of funds exchanged per day, or things like that.

e) Now, compare the null and alternative hypotheses by calculating the Proportional Reduction in Error (PRE) statistic. Does the alternative hypothesis predict better than the null? If so, by how much? (*Hint:* See Chapter 4 to review calculating PRE.)

_____

_____

Table 11.6 shows the same set of cases but instead explains signing behavior by looking at whether states were already at or near compliant behavior when they signed. We again examine all available state-years. The variable "Prior Restriction" indicates whether a state had restrictions on its current account in the year prior to the observation. Because this variable is lagged—that is to say, it takes on the value of the year prior to it—its value is missing for the first year that a state enters the dataset. This accounts for the smaller number of cases in this analysis.

TABLE 11.6

Article VIII Signing and Prior Compliance

		Article VIII		
		0	**1**	**Total**
Prior Restriction	**0**	554	1344	1898
	1	1793	477	2270
	Total	2347	1821	4168

f) Which school's argument does this table test? _____

g) Eyeball the data. Do the data suggest that prior compliance influences signing? What makes you think so? (*Hint:* Which row indicates prior compliance?)

_____

_____

h) Highlight the cells of Table 11.6 that show correct predictions by the null hypothesis. Then calculate what proportion of the cases the null hypothesis correctly predicts.

i) Highlight the cells of Table 11.6 that show correct predictions by the new alternative hypothesis: that prior compliance leads to signing. Then calculate the proportion of observations that the alternative hypothesis correctly predicts.

j)   Compare this new alternative hypothesis, H_2, to the null hypothesis of the modal outcome. Using the proportion you calculated in part h of this exercise, calculate the PRE for the prior compliance hypothesis. Does the alternative hypothesis predict better than the null? If so, by how much?

_____

_____

k)   Compare your two sets of results in parts e and j of this exercise. Which argument is a better predictor? How do you know? How much does the better theory improve on the predictions of the weaker one? (*Hint:* Think about how we can determine how much better one theory is than another.)

_____

_____

_____

Comparing the Arguments: Who Complies?

Let's consider the issue now of who complies with commitments. Remember, compliance here is "Not Restrict."
Table 11.7 explains restrictions on current accounts by examining whether states have signed Article VIII.

TABLE 11.7
Current Account Restriction and Article VIII Signing

		Current Account Restriction		
		0	**1**	**Total**
Article VIII	**0**	598	1890	2488
	1	1374	483	1857
	Total	1972	2373	4345

l)   Which school's argument does this table test? _____

m) Which variable here is the independent variable? Which is the dependent variable?

Independent = _____   Dependent = _____

n)   Eyeball the data. Do the data suggest that signing influences compliance? What makes you think so?

_____

_____

o) What is the modal outcome in Table 11.7? What is the new null hypothesis? Highlight the cells of Table 11.7 that show correct predictions by the null hypothesis. Then calculate what proportion of the cases the null hypothesis correctly predicts.

_____

_____

p) Using a second highlighter in a different color, indicate which cells are correct predictions by the alternative hypothesis. Then calculate what proportion of the cases the alternative hypothesis correctly predicts.

q) Now, compare the null and alternative hypotheses by calculating the PRE. Does the alternative hypothesis predict better than the null? If so, by how much?

_____

_____

Table 11.8 explains restrictions on a state's current account behavior by examining states' prior compliance before signing. Again, the total number of observations is lower because of the presence of the lagged variable.

TABLE 11.8

Current Compliance and Prior Compliance

		Restriction		
		0	1	Total
Prior Restriction	**0**	1772	126	1898
	1	139	2131	2270
	Total	1911	2257	4168

r) Which school's argument does this table test? _____

s) Eyeball the data. Do the data suggest that prior compliance influences compliance? What makes you think so?

_____

_____

t)   What is the modal outcome in our new table? What is the new null hypothesis? Highlight the cells of Table 11.8 that show correct predictions by the null hypothesis. Then calculate what proportion of the cases the null hypothesis correctly predicts.

_____

_____

u)   Highlight the cells of Table 11.8 that show correct predictions by the new alternative hypothesis, that prior compliance leads to signing. Then calculate the proportion of observations that the alternative hypothesis correctly predicts.

v)   Compare this new alternative hypothesis, H_2, to the null hypothesis. Using the proportion you calculated in part n of this exercise, calculate the PRE for the H_2. Does the alternative hypothesis predict better than the null? If so, by how much?

_____

_____

w)   Compare your two sets of results in parts q and v of this exercise. Which argument is a better predictor? How do you know? How much does the better theory improve on the predictions of the weaker one?

_____

_____

_____

EXTENSIONS

Exercise 11-7.   *Exploring Hypotheses about International Institutions*

Using your college's or university's library resources, obtain a copy of "The Rational Design of International Institutions," by Barbara Koremenos, Charles Lipson, and Duncan Snidal, from *International Organization* 55, 1 (Autumn 2001): 761–799. Skim the article, then use that information to help you determine where to read more closely to answer these questions.

a) Koremenos and other contributors to the special issue of *International Organization* (in which this article appears) define international institutions as both formal organizations and informal regimes. International organizations have observable characteristics: they have offices and budgets and staff. Regimes and other informal institutions, on the other hand, do not. If you were going to design a study to test some of the article's conjectures about rational design, you would want to include these informal organizations in the sample. What kinds of observable effects would informal institutions have? In other words, how would you know an informal institution existed so that you could include it?

_____

_____

_____

_____

_____

b) For each of the international organizations listed below, identify two of the article's conjectures that appear to be supported by that organization's design. You may identify the conjectures as C1, M3, etc.; see the helpful list on page 797 of the article. You may need to do some background research on these organizations to respond; helpful links are on the text's Web site at http://bdm.cqpress.com.

1. The United Nations (UN) _____

2. The Organization of Petroleum Exporting Countries (OPEC) _____

3. The Organization for Economic Co-Operation and Development (OECD) _____

4. The European Union (EU) _____

5. The Association of South East Asian Nations (ASEAN) Regional Forum (ARF) _____

6. The Shanghai Cooperation Organization _____

Exercise 11-8. *Cooperation and Non-Compliance*

a) We discussed above the fairly prominent argument that claims compliance with international agreements is high not because agreements are binding or because states fear punishment for defection, but because states will not sign agreements to do things that they do not already have interests or incentives to do anyway even without an agreement. If this argument is true, why might we still see noncompliance? Brainstorm two or three reasons and explain briefly why or how each might cause defection.

_____

_____

_____

_____

b) For each of the reasons for defection that you identified in part a of this exercise, identify a way that states could mitigate that source of defection. Think about issues of institutional design like those Koremenos et al. identified as independent variables.

_____

_____

_____

_____

_____

_____

_____

c) You want to conduct research about the causes of defection you just proposed in part a. You have identified a set of cases of defection, and you now wish to identify which of your hypothesized causes contributed most to each defection. Consider your list of proposed causes. For each, identify one or two observable indicators that would exist or conditions that would be true if that particular cause were at work in a case.

_____

_____

_____

_____

_____

_____

_____

_____

_____

_____

_____

_____

_____